POWER FOR KINGDOM PROSPERITY

Biblical Principles for Lasting Wealth and Impact

DR. JOHN ANIEMEKE

Power for Kingdom Prosperity

Paperback ISBN: 978-1-965593-82-0

Published by Cornerstone Publishing

A Division of Cornerstone Creativity Group LLC
Info@thecornerstonepublishers.com
www.thecornerstonepublishers.com

Author's Contact

To book the author to speak at your next event or to order bulk copies of this book, please, use the information below:

janiemeke@yahoo.com

Printed in the United States of America.

This book is dedicated to the Almighty God, the Source -ABBA , our provider and the owner and giver of all good gifts in this life and eternity.

I pray it blesses you and becomes a spring board to a life full of prosperity; Spirit, Soul & Body. Amen!

CONTENTS

INTRODUCTION

Divine prosperity has always been one of the most misunderstood and misrepresented topics in Christendom. While some believe that to be poor is to be holy, others uphold a version of prosperity that is obsessed with materialism and detached from God's character. Caught between these two extremes, many Christians are confused and disadvantaged. This anomaly is what this book was inspired to address.

Prosperity, as presented in Scripture, is not a pursuit of luxury or indulgence. It is a covenant reality, entrenched in God's desire to establish His will on earth through His people. From Abraham to David, from Joseph to the early Church, we see a consistent pattern: when God wants to advance His agenda, He entrusts resources to those who are yielded to His will.

Power for Kingdom Prosperity is a prophetic call to align your life with this operation of Heaven's economy. It is a call to break free from the limitations of earthly systems and shackling beliefs, and step into the supernatural flow of provision that belongs to every covenant child of God.

The reason many believers are living beneath their spiritual and financial potential is because they have not been taught how to access what is already theirs. This book will take you deep into the spiritual truths that govern Kingdom wealth. You will learn how to apply covenant principles, activate prosperity promises, dismantle satanic resistance, and cultivate the mindset required to steward abundance with integrity and purpose.

The revelations here are not reserved for ministers or entrepreneurs. They are for every believer who understands that their life is an assignment. Whether you are called to transform lives, build churches, fund missions, raise a godly family, or influence communities, you need resources. And those resources must be accessed God's way. The power to prosper is not found in worldly schemes; it is found in covenant commitment, spiritual sensitivity, and faithful stewardship.

God is raising a generation of believers who will not only carry His presence but also wield His provision. The days of Christianity marked by spiritual passion but financial deprivation are coming to an end. The Kingdom of God is advancing, and it requires men and women who understand that prosperity is not a distraction from holiness, but a dimension of divine purpose.

PART 1

Foundational Truths About Kingdom Prosperity

1

WHY KINGDOM PROSPERITY?

"God's desire for prosperity is rooted in His desire for you to live free from lack, stress, and dependency."

– Creflo Dollar

Prosperity, in its most basic sense, is the state of being successful, wealthy and comfortable. From this economic perspective, to be prosperous is to enjoy material wealth, possessions, and financial security. These can include income, property, investments, and other assets that contribute to a good standard of living. The word comes from the Latin *prosperitas*, meaning "favorable outcome" or "success", and is rooted in *prosperus*, which means "agreeable to one's wishes".

However, it is important to distinguish between earthly prosperity and Kingdom prosperity - that is, the prosperity that belongs to God's Kingdom and is intended for His children. This distinction must be made from the outset of this life-changing journey, so you can clearly understand what God truly desires for you and how you can access it.

Interestingly, the fact that both earthly and Kingdom prosperity share the word "prosperity" means they do overlap in certain areas. Before we focus fully on what Kingdom prosperity entails, let's briefly explore where the two intersect.

First, both forms of prosperity involve having sufficient financial and material resources for personal comfort and the ability to help others. More importantly, financial prosperity is available to anyone, believer or unbeliever, who applies the right principles for building and sustaining wealth. These principles include hard work, strategic planning, wise spending, deliberate saving, and smart investing.

Scripture supports this in several places. In Genesis 8:22 (NLT), God declares, *"As long as the earth remains, there will be planting and harvest…"* This is a universal law that applies to all of humanity. Similarly, Proverbs 22:29 (KJV) says, *"Seest thou a man diligent in his business? he shall stand before kings; he shall not stand before mean men."*

Note that it doesn't say, "Seest thou a believer…" It's a principle that applies broadly; faithful diligence attracts increase.

Even though God grants special favor to His people, Christ clearly explains that God does not discriminate in dispensing certain blessings. Matthew 5:45 (KJV) says, *"He maketh his sun to rise on the evil and on the good, and sendeth rain on the just and on the unjust."*

In ancient Israel, a largely agrarian society, sunlight and rain were essential for occupational success and, by extension, prosperity. By using this imagery, Jesus was emphasizing that God has made available to all the basic ingredients for success. God Himself affirms this principle in Isaiah 55:10 (NLT): *"The rain and snow come down from the heavens and stay on the ground to water the earth. They cause the grain to grow, producing seed for the farmer and bread for the hungry."*

Notice the generality in the language; there's no mention of the farmer's religious status. Whether the farmer is a Christian or not, the seed will grow if he sows and cultivates it diligently. The implication is that prosperity, at its base level, follows laws and principles that are available to all.

NO EXEMPTIONS FROM PROSPERITY PRINCIPLES

On the flip side, even believers can miss out on prosperity if they ignore or violate these fundamental principles. Proverbs 10:4 (NKJV) warns, *"He who has a slack hand becomes poor, but the hand of the diligent makes rich."* Proverbs 12:24 (NLT) advises, *"Work hard and become a leader; be lazy and become a slave."* And in Proverbs 24:30–31 (NLT), Solomon recounts: *"I walked by the field of a lazy person, the vineyard of one with no common sense. I saw that it was overgrown with nettles. It was covered with weeds, and its walls were broken down."*

These verses speak in absolute terms. Whether or not you're a believer, laziness leads to lack, and diligence attracts increase. This helps explain why some Christians struggle financially while unbelievers seem to thrive. Often, it's not about spirituality, destiny, demonic opposition, or divine timing; it may simply be about one's approach to the laws of prosperity.

In other words, not everything in the Kingdom hinges on spiritual warfare or divine intervention. Many outcomes follow natural laws. For instance, while God has promised healing and health, violating natural health principles can still lead to disease. Also, while

He promises success, failing to prepare often results in failure. In essence, God does not override responsibility with miracles where diligence is required.

Sadly, many believers fall short in the area of practical knowledge and disciplined application, causing them to live far below God's intentions for them. This grieves the heart of God. In Isaiah 5:13 (KJV), He laments: *"Therefore my people are gone into captivity, because they have no knowledge: and their honorable men are famished, and their multitude dried up with thirst."*

Jesus echoed this sentiment in Luke 16:8, after telling the parable of the shrewd manager: *"For the children of this world are in their generation wiser than the children of light."* This was not an endorsement of dishonesty, but a call to strategic thinking and foresight. Believers are called to be as intentional, as prepared, and as thoughtful as the world, and even more so. Faith is not an excuse for sloppiness. Faith without works is dead (James 2:17).

That is the core message we will be exploring in the second part of this exposition. Our God is not only a covenant-keeping God; He is also a God of strategy. He will not do for us what He has already given us the power and wisdom to do. He expects us to partner with Him, playing our part in the covenant of abundance.

As we go deeper into the subject of Kingdom prosperity - which is a supernatural and elevated dimension of prosperity - keep this in mind: God's provision does not cancel personal responsibility. Kingdom prosperity does not exempt us from diligence, planning, or wise stewardship. Rather, it calls us into a realm where our human efforts are guided, accelerated, and multiplied by divine grace.

NATURE OF KINGDOM PROSPERITY

So, what exactly is Kingdom prosperity? In a broad sense, it is the divine empowerment to flourish in every area of your life (spiritually, financially, physically, and otherwise) for the fulfillment of God's purpose and the advancement of His Kingdom on earth. This is what the Scripture refers to in 3 John 1:2: *"Beloved, I wish above all things that thou mayest prosper and be in health, even as thy soul prospereth."* Again, Proverbs 10:22 (NLT) says, *"The blessing of the LORD makes a person rich, and he adds no sorrow with it."*

What this reveals is that the prosperity God bestows on His children is one that knows no lack or limitation. It brings complete wholeness—so that you are thriving, joyful, and fulfilled in your spirit, soul, body, relationships, purpose, finances, and aspirations. It is the shalom experience, characterized not only by abundance and peace that surpasses all understanding but also by uncommon favor, soundness of body and mind, fruitfulness, fervency in spirit, and unlimited impact.

Scripture gives us an example of how Abraham flourished in Kingdom prosperity even in his old age: *"And Abraham was old, and well stricken in age: and the LORD had blessed Abraham in all things"* (Genesis 24:1). Solomon also enjoyed this shalom experience and testified: *"But now the LORD my God has given me peace on every side; I have no enemies, and all is well"* (1 Kings 5:4).

Hallelujah! What a remarkable declaration. And this is the same testimony God desires for you, as He invites you to savor the all-round prosperity of His Kingdom. He says to you: *"You would be fed with the finest of wheat; with honey from the rock I would satisfy you"* (Psalm 81:16).

This phrase reflects God's promise of provision and abundance. In biblical times, wheat was a staple food, symbolizing sustenance and prosperity. The "finest of wheat" suggests not just basic provision, but the best quality, indicating God's desire to give His people more than the bare essentials. Honey in ancient Israel symbolized delight and abundance, often associated with the Promised Land described as "a land flowing with milk and honey." The mention of "honey from the rock" is especially striking, suggesting miraculous provision from unlikely places, much like the water that gushed from the rock (Exodus 17:6). This imagery powerfully illustrates God's ability to provide for His people in seemingly impossible situations.

NO CONTRADICTION

Note that there is no contradiction in saying that Kingdom prosperity comes from divine empowerment and, at the same time, involves intentional effort and responsibility on our part. This becomes clearer when you understand, first of all, that Kingdom prosperity includes not just tangible assets like financial and material wealth but also intangible riches such as sound health, fullness of joy, peace of mind, and a deep sense of contentment and fulfillment; things that no amount of earthly riches can provide. This is evident in the many tragic stories of seemingly wealthy individuals who lived miserably or even took their own lives due to frustration and deep-seated emptiness.

Secondly, even in terms of tangible assets, while those outside the Kingdom rely solely on personal effort and natural laws to obtain results, Kingdom citizens receive supernatural guidance and divine support in their efforts, and the results are often exponential! Consider the example of Isaac in Genesis 26:12–14 (KJV): *"Then Isaac sowed in that land, and received in the same year a hundredfold: and the LORD blessed him. And the man waxed great, and went forward, and grew until he became very great: for he had possession of flocks, and possession of herds, and great store of servants: and the Philistines envied him."* Paul the Apostle also shared his experience of ministerial prosperity: *"I have planted, Apollos watered; but God gave the increase. So then neither is he that planteth any thing, neither he that watereth; but God that giveth the increase"* (1 Corinthians 3:6–7).

In both cases, human efforts were present, but the miraculous outcomes revealed that it was ultimately God orchestrating the results. The example of Peter and his companions in John 21:1–6 is even more striking. They had been toiling all night using natural methods, drawing on their professional expertise as fishermen, but they caught nothing. Then Christ appeared and instructed them: *"Cast the net on the right side of the ship, and ye shall find"* (John 21:6). They obeyed, and immediately, *"they were not able to draw it for the multitude of fishes."* That is the distinguishing mark of Kingdom prosperity.

Again, in contrast to worldly prosperity, which is often pursued at the expense of the soul, Kingdom prosperity flows from the inner prosperity of the soul (3 John 2). It begins within and overflows outward. That is why its pursuit is marked by dependence on God, righteous labor, integrity, obedience, and generous giving. Earthly prosperity, by contrast, often depends on exploitation, manipulation, shortcuts, and the philosophy of "the end justifies the means."

Kingdom prosperity also differs from worldly prosperity in terms of ownership, purpose, motivation, and fruit. Kingdom prosperity belongs to the King of kings and is entrusted to His children for stewardship. *"The earth is the LORD's, and everything in it…"* (Psalm 24:1). And the beautiful thing is that Kingdom-minded people acknowledge this truth, unlike the possessors of worldly wealth who attribute their success to personal strength or cunning, just as Nebuchadnezzar did in Daniel 4:30.

In purpose, Kingdom prosperity is geared toward advancing God's Kingdom, blessing others, and fulfilling divine agenda, whereas worldly prosperity tends to prioritize personal comfort, status, and indulgence. Moreover, since Kingdom prosperity is received from God, His children are neither anxious nor desperate to accumulate or preserve it, even as they diligently steward it. They handle it with a deep sense of gratitude and responsibility, resulting in lives marked by joy, peace, generosity, contentment and leaving behind a transgenerational legacy.

By contrast, many who pursue earthly prosperity are driven by greed, pride, or a need for self-validation. Their identity is often tied to their wealth, which traps them in cycles of pressure, comparison, and anxiety about securing and multiplying their riches. In the end, their legacy is often short-lived and perishable.

Now you can see why only Kingdom prosperity truly matters to God and bears His approval. Any prosperity lacking these Kingdom elements is not only worthless in His sight, but also dangerous to the soul and potentially damning. This is revealed in the parable of the rich fool in Luke 12:13–21, which Christ concludes with these sobering words: *"But God said to him, 'You fool! This very night your life will be demanded from you. Then who will get what you have prepared for yourself?' This is how it will be with whoever stores up things for themselves but is not rich toward God."*

THE FINANCIAL DIMENSION OF KINGDOM PROSPERITY

One poignant observation I've made over the years is this: while many believers seem fairly conversant with the various dimensions of Kingdom prosperity, a significant number are either ignorant of the financial dimension or choose to ignore it altogether. The consequences have been many, and deeply concerning.

For this reason, the rest of our exposition throughout this book will address this gap by exploring the principles, pathways, and practices of Kingdom financial prosperity, and how we can enjoy it to the full.

As an overview, financial prosperity in God's Kingdom is the divinely enabled ability to acquire, manage, and multiply financial resources in alignment with God's principles and purposes. The goal is to meet personal and family needs, bless others, and advance His Kingdom, without compromising spiritual integrity, contentment, or eternal priorities.

Let me briefly break this down for you:

- Financial prosperity in God's Kingdom is not just from hustle or intellect; it's grace-backed. God Himself gives His children power to get wealth (Deuteronomy 8:18).
- This power is exercised through righteous means—work, creativity, business, and investment, not through fraud, shortcuts, or compromise.
- Kingdom wealth comes with the responsibility of providing for personal and family needs (1 Timothy 5:8), living within one's means, impacting God's Kingdom and humanity, and leaving an inheritance (Proverbs 13:22)

- The wealth is managed through budgeting, stewardship, avoiding waste and debt, and making wise financial decisions.

- It is multiplied through godly strategies, like saving, investing, and reinvesting in Kingdom ventures and productive enterprises.

- It is sustained through absolute trust in God and godliness (Matthew 6:33; Proverbs 11:1), generosity (Luke 6:38), tithing and giving (Malachi 3:10), avoiding greed (Luke 12:15), and planning wisely (Proverbs 21:5).

- It is viewed as a means of blessing others - giving to the poor, helping those in need, sponsoring causes that uplift communities; and promoting Kingdom work - supporting churches, missionaries, and ministries; funding outreach, education, and relief efforts; as well as creating structures that reflect God's justice and mercy

- It keeps the heart rooted in God, not in mammon (Matthew 6:24).

- It seeks treasure in heaven, not just on earth (Matthew 6:19–20).

In a nutshell, Kingdom prosperity is neither a poverty that glorifies lack nor a luxury that glorifies self. It is a life of purpose-filled provision, where God is glorified, people are blessed, and eternity is prioritized.

Let's now unpack the details of this powerful revelation in the subsequent chapters.

2

PROSPERITY IS YOUR HERITAGE

"God is the source of my supply. His riches flow to me freely, copiously, and abundantly. All my financial and other needs are met at every moment of time and point of space; there is always a divine surplus."

- Joseph Murphy

This is a fundamental truth that must be firmly established in your mind if you want to access and abound in Kingdom prosperity. In fact, it is your foundational step into experiencing Kingdom wealth. Scripture declares that when you know the truth, the truth will set you free (John 8:32).

The revelations in this chapter will accomplish three things in your life. One, it will liberate you from living below your Kingdom privilege of abundance. Two, it will show you how to enjoy this privilege without losing your soul. Three, it will help you to maximize your God-given wealth the Kingdom way.

I mentioned in the previous chapter that one very common area in which many believers live far below their Kingdom privileges is prosperity. While this is sometimes because of ignorance of what God has made available for them, the more common reason is the demonization of this divine provision. For far too long, prosperity has been condemned by some preachers and believers as unspiritual and materialistic, while poverty is glamorized as God's standard tool for building strong and steadfast believers.

Let me quickly point out some of the common misconceptions about Kingdom prosperity that continue to keep some believers bound in scarcity, when they should be thriving in abundance.

1. *"Wealth is always worldly or evil."*

There's a persistent belief that financial blessing is inherently corrupt or spiritually dangerous. In other words, it's "holier" to be poor, since prosperity is assumed to have a corrupting influence.

2. *"God only cares about our spiritual life."*

Some assume that God is concerned only with the salvation of the soul and not with financial or material well-being.

3. *"Poverty and hardship are always part of God's will."*

Many believe that Christians are called to suffer lack and financial difficulty as part of spiritual formation.

4. *"Poverty makes you humble and closer to God."*

Some equate material lack with humility and godliness, assuming that the less you have, the more spiritual you are. The story of the rich man and Lazarus is often misused to support this claim.

5. *"Seeking financial blessing means you're greedy or carnal."*

There's often suspicion toward Christians who talk openly about finances, as though any focus on money is automatically motivated by greed or materialism.

6. *"Jesus was poor, so believers must be poor."*

It is argued that since Jesus and His disciples lived modestly, Christians must embrace poverty as a sign of true holiness.

7. *"Prosperity distracts from focusing on heaven and eternity."*

   Some believe that any interest in financial blessing undermines the believer's focus on eternal life and Kingdom priorities.

GOD'S ACTUAL WILL FOR YOU

Contrary to these gloomy claims, Scripture paints a completely different picture, one in which Kingdom wealth is not just part of your inheritance but something God takes seriously. Let's revisit two verses we looked at earlier. 3 John 1:2 (KJV) says, *"Beloved, I wish above all things that thou mayest prosper and be in health, even as thy soul prospereth."* Deuteronomy 8:18 is even more emphatic: *"But thou shalt remember the Lord thy God: for it is he that giveth thee power to get wealth, that he may establish his covenant."*

Now, this is a mighty revelation! It is God who gives His children the ability to create wealth. We will explore the first part of that verse later on, but for now, let's dig deeper into this profound truth. If wealth were inherently evil or dangerous, why would a loving God want to ensnare or endanger His own children? If prosperity were inherently corrupting, why would God grant it? Clearly, this tells you something about the actual truth of the matter.

But there are even more striking revelations. Psalm 35:27 declares, *"Let the Lord be magnified, which hath pleasure in the prosperity of his servant."* Also, Proverbs 10:22 affirms, *"The blessing of the Lord, it maketh rich, and he addeth no sorrow with it."* And for those who may think this is just an Old Testament theme, 2 Corinthians 9:8 (KJV) adds: *"And God is able to make all grace abound toward you; that ye, always having all sufficiency in all things, may abound to every good work."*

These verses and many others clearly show that true prosperity is part of your Kingdom heritage. It's not a man-made idea; it's God's idea. It's firmly rooted in Scripture and woven throughout His covenant with His people. In fact, Jesus spoke more about money than He did about heaven or hell. That alone tells you that the prosperity and financial stewardship of God's children occupy a major place in His divine agenda.

Essentially, while salvation and redemption through Christ primarily deliver us from the bondage of sin, they also liberate us from every other work of the devil, including poverty. 1 John 3:8 (KJV) declares: "*…For this purpose the Son of God was manifested, that he might destroy the works of the devil.*"

Notice the use of the plural "works", and not just "work." This matters because the damage Satan did to humanity in Eden wasn't limited to sin alone. He also introduced other distortions into human experience, such as sickness, shame, oppression, and lack.

Remember that before man was created, everything he needed for survival and abundance was already provided. Man was created into an atmosphere of abundance. As long as man remained in unbroken fellowship with God, there was no record of insufficiency. The moment man was disconnected from God, lack entered the human story. This proves that lack is one of the "works" of the devil. It follows, then, that being reconciled to God through salvation also repositions us into our original state of divine abundance. In other words, there is a provision for prosperity within the full salvation package. No wonder Psalm 1:3 (KJV) says the true believer is *"like a tree planted by the rivers of water, that bringeth forth his fruit in his season; his leaf also shall not wither; and whatsoever he doeth shall prosper."*

Isn't this remarkable? God describes the one who abides in Him as a tree "planted"—that is, intentionally positioned and rooted in divine abundance, with constant access to spiritual and physical nourishment. A tree by a river never fears drought. Its leaves do not wither because its source is not circumstantial but supernatural. Likewise, the life of abundance that salvation brings is not tied to your background, job, or the economy. It's anchored in God's inexhaustible supply. *"But my God shall supply all your need according to his riches in glory by Christ Jesus"* (Philippians 4:19).

Even more, the verse in Psalm 1:3 specifically promises all-round prosperity: *"And whatsoever he doeth shall prosper."* This means that cultivating a thriving relationship with God automatically empowers you to succeed in whatever job, business, calling, or venture He has led you into. This is not wishful thinking but a divine assurance. Moreover, the use of the word *"shall"* and not *"may"* shows that this is a guaranteed blessing for every child of God who believes and activates it by faith.

In the end, it's a choice between believing what God has said about your prosperity or accepting a man-made, poverty-affirming gospel. As Paul asked in Romans 3:3–4 (NKJV): *"For what if some did not believe? Will their unbelief make the faithfulness of God without effect? Certainly not! Indeed, let God be true but every man a liar."*

A COVENANT RIGHT, NOT A CARNAL DREAM

Let's go even deeper. Prosperity, as intended by God, is not about vanity, greed, or self-centered accumulation. Rather, it is a covenant provision, a right secured through the redemptive work of Christ and revealed throughout Scripture. Galatians 3:13–14 declares: *"Christ hath redeemed us from the curse of the law, being made a curse for us… that the blessing of Abraham might come on the Gentiles through Jesus Christ."*

One key element of *"the blessing of Abraham,"* as we saw earlier, was material and financial prosperity: *"And Abram was very rich in cattle, in silver, and in gold"* (Genesis 13:2). God Himself initiated Abraham's prosperity; it wasn't driven by Abraham's ambition. God's blessing made him prosper. And according to Galatians 3:29: *"If ye be Christ's, then are ye Abraham's seed, and heirs according to the promise."*

This means that as we enter into a covenant relationship with God through Christ, we automatically become heirs (fellow partakers) of the same blessings God gave to Abraham. Why then should you possess the faith of Abraham but not the corresponding prosperity?

To further show the scope of the prosperity Abraham enjoyed, and which Scripture says you are entitled to, understand this: Abraham was not just rich; he was wealthy. There's a difference. Being "rich" often refers to having a high income or plenty of money at the moment, usually linked to a lifestyle of spending and consumption. On the other hand, being "wealthy" implies possessing long-term, income-generating assets (such as real estate or investments) that provide enduring financial security.

The key distinction lies in net worth, which is calculated as assets minus liabilities. A person may be rich but have little or no net worth if they spend everything they earn. Wealth, however, is sustainable and transferable. While the rich may accumulate depreciating items like flashy cars or designer handbags, wealth often comprises appreciating or legacy assets, those that can be passed on to future generations.

Indeed, the Abrahamic blessing was not limited to Abraham. It included generational wealth. Scripture shows the same prosperity extended to Isaac, his son: *"And the Lord blessed him. And the man waxed great, and went forward, and grew until he became very great: for he had possession of flocks, and possession of herds, and great store of servants: and the Philistines envied him"* (Genesis 26:12–14).

Likewise, Jacob, Isaac's son, *"became very wealthy, with large flocks of sheep and goats, female and male servants, and many camels and donkeys"* (Genesis 30:43, NLT).

Beyond the patriarchs, Boaz - the upright man who married Ruth - is described as *"a man of great wealth"* (Ruth 2:1, NKJV). Job, too, is described as being so wealthy that he became "*the greatest man among all the people of the East*" (Job 1:1–3). Yet, this same man was *"blameless and upright; he feared God and shunned evil."* Incredible!

King David, whom God described as a man after His own heart, also enjoyed this covenant prosperity. The Scripture records: *"He died at a good old age, having enjoyed long life, wealth, and honor"* (1 Chronicles 29:28). David himself testified that such abundance wasn't unique to him. He said, *"I was young and now I am old, yet have I never seen the righteous forsaken, nor his seed begging bread"* (Psalm 37:25).

So, again, I ask: where did this "poverty gospel" that says righteousness must go hand in hand with wretchedness come from? It certainly didn't originate in the New Testament because Scripture also testifies of prosperous New Testament believers. Joanna, Susanna, and many other affluent followers were the human vessels God used to finance Jesus' ministry (Luke 8:3). Joseph of Arimathea, who arranged for Jesus' burial, is described as *"a rich man"* (Matthew 27:57). Lydia of

Thyatira, a dealer in purple cloth, a luxury reserved for royalty and the elite, was clearly wealthy. Yet she embraced the gospel and used her resources to host Paul and his team (Acts 16:14–15).

Even Paul the Apostle acknowledged the existence of wealthy believers in Ephesus, a thriving port city known for commerce and culture. Not only did he refrain from condemning their wealth, but he also affirmed that God was its source and instructed them on its proper use: *"Charge them that are rich in this world, that they be not highminded, nor trust in uncertain riches, but in the living God, who giveth us richly all things to enjoy"* (1 Timothy 6:17).

These examples show that Kingdom wealth is both scriptural and attainable. More importantly, they prove that we can be both prosperous and deeply spiritual, if we understand the essence of Kingdom wealth and live accordingly. In fact, they suggest that prosperity, rightly understood and managed, can make us more effective in Kingdom expansion.

We will explore the implications of this in greater detail later in this chapter. But first, there is a critical question that demands deeper reflection.

DOES POVERTY IMPLY OR IMPROVE SPIRITUALITY?

I mentioned earlier that some Christians believe poverty is a mark of humility or piety. Yet, as widespread as this idea is, it has no biblical foundation. Scripture never praises lack or scarcity as a virtue. In fact, poverty is often depicted as a condition from which God desires to deliver His people.. 1 Samuel 2:8 (JKV), for example, says: *"He raiseth up the poor out of the dust, and lifteth up the beggar from the dunghill, to set them among princes, and to make them inherit the throne of glory: for the pillars of the earth are the Lord's, and he hath set the world upon them."* Interestingly, Psalm 113:7–8 says exactly the same thing: *"He raiseth up the poor out of the dust, and lifteth the needy out of the dunghill; that he may set him with princes."*

If poverty were meant to make us more spiritual, God wouldn't be so invested in lifting His people out of its dunghill and placing them among princes. Truth is, neither poverty nor prosperity determines our relationship with God; it's a matter of personal decision and devotion. That's why Paul the apostle could declare: *"I know both how to be abased, and I know how to abound: every where and in all things I am instructed both to be full and to be hungry, both to abound and to suffer need"* (Philippians 4:12).

Without mastering the spiritual discipline of trusting God in every season, neither abundance nor lack can guarantee spiritual depth. Just as prosperity can ensnare an unstable soul in pride, indulgence, or self-reliance, so also can poverty breed envy, bitterness, despair, or compromise.

Some people cite the story of Lazarus and the rich man (Luke 16:19–31) to argue that poverty implies or improves spirituality. But that interpretation distorts the actual message. Jesus never said Lazarus went to heaven because he was poor. The name Lazarus means "God has helped," suggesting he trusted in God despite his suffering. The rich man, by contrast, lived in luxury and ignored Lazarus's plight. His downfall wasn't his wealth; it was his selfishness, indifference, and lack of compassion. Even in torment, he saw Lazarus as beneath him, asking Abraham to send him like a servant.

This mirrors other biblical warnings: the rich fool (Luke 12:13–21), the rich young ruler (Luke 18:18–25), and the vivid metaphor of a camel passing through the eye of a needle (Luke 18:25). In each case, the issue was not money, but misplaced trust in riches, neglect of the poor, self-centered living, and an unwillingness to surrender material attachments, unlike Abraham, who offered Isaac without hesitation.

And what of Jesus Himself, who lived without wealth? It's critical to understand that He chose a path of detachment, not because poverty was inherently righteous, but because it was necessary for His mission of humility and sacrifice. It would be wrong to assume that poverty is therefore a requirement for godliness, just as it would be wrong to conclude that singleness is a universal mandate simply because Jesus wasn't married.

Indeed, the Bible makes it clear that Jesus took on a life of poverty for our sake—to lift us, not impoverish us: "*For ye know the grace of our Lord Jesus Christ, that, though he was rich, yet for your sakes he became poor, that ye through his poverty might be rich*" (2 Corinthians 8:9).

It's time to stop allowing fear, guilt, or theological distortion to confine us to substandard living. God is still in the business of raising spiritually mature, economically empowered believers who will transform families, communities, and nations.

Let's proceed to see the exact reasons God wants us prosperous.

3

PURPOSE OF KINGDOM PROSPERITY

"The King only gives resources to the colony to accomplish His purposes."

– Dr. Myles Munroe

As noted earlier, prosperity in God's Kingdom is always tied to purpose. God doesn't bless His children simply so they can live lavishly or selfishly; He blesses us so we can glorify Him and fulfil His agenda on earth.

Scripture is unequivocally clear that Kingdom wealth is not a trophy to be hoarded or flaunted, but a tool to achieve specific Kingdom objectives. Let's revisit two verses that emphasize this truth. 2 Corinthians 9:8 (NLT) assures us: "*And God will generously provide all you need. Then you will always have everything you need and plenty left over to share with others.*" 1 Timothy 6:17–19 declares: "*Command those who are rich in this present world… to do good, to be rich in good deeds, and to be generous and willing to share. In this way they will lay up treasure for themselves as a firm foundation for the coming age, so that they may take hold of the life that is truly life.*"

From these and other scriptural revelations, it's clear that God prospers His children so that the following Kingdom goals can be achieved:

1. The General Wellbeing of His Children

While we serve and reverence God as the Almighty, He is primarily a loving Father to His children. This is why Jesus used the word *"Father"* more than any other description or name for Him. Once you grasp this truth, you begin to understand that God's desire to prosper us naturally flows from His parental heart.

Just as earthly parents find joy in their children's growth, flourishing, and stability, so does God take pleasure in the wellbeing of His own. Psalm 35:27 affirms this: "*Let the Lord be magnified, who has pleasure in the prosperity of His servant.*"

Even the most hardened human hearts often soften toward their children and go to great lengths to ensure they are well provided for. This is why Christ asks: "*If you then, being evil, know how to give good gifts to your children, how much more will your Father in heaven give good things…*" (Matthew 7:11).

This shows that prosperity is a fundamental part of God's character and His dealings with His children. It's an expression of His caring and nurturing heart. Like every doting parent, He wants you to be happy as you enjoy the fruits of your labor. He wants you prioritize self-care - to eat well, look good, live a productive life, relax and go on vacations - even as your soul flourishes. "*When God gives someone wealth and possessions, and the ability to enjoy them, to accept their lot and be happy in their toil—this is a gift of God.*" (Ecclesiastes 5:19)

Beyond physical wellbeing, Kingdom prosperity is also meant to help us fulfill our personal callings and destinies. Many callings, whether in ministry, education, business, or the arts, require resources for full expression. Ecclesiastes 10:19 (KJV) says: "*Money answereth all things.*"

This doesn't mean money replaces spiritual matters, but it does acknowledge that many God-given visions need funding to become reality. Kingdom wealth empowers us to launch new ministries or initiatives, start businesses or nonprofits aligned with God's purposes, or pursue education or training that equips us for greater impact.

In short, while a lack of financial resources can hinder personal and Kingdom visions, Kingdom wealth removes such barriers.

2. Freedom to serve God without financial anxiety

Kingdom prosperity is not about the ability to afford luxuries, but freedom from constant worry about basic needs. In Luke 1:73-75 (KJV), Simeon the prophet declares: "*The oath which he sware to our father Abraham, That he would grant unto us, that we being delivered out of the hand of our enemies might serve him without fear, In holiness and righteousness before him, all the days of our life.*"

Poverty is one of the most formidable enemies of the believer. It seeks to limit our wellness, peace, joy and impact by subjecting us to a persistent sense of worry, fear, or unease about our financial situation. While we are exhorted to shun worry and anxiety over our daily needs, this becomes an uphill task as bills mount, expenses increase, debts pile up and emergencies arise without adequate income or financial resources to meet them.

Here is a good example of this in the Scripture: "*The wife of a man from the company of the prophets cried out to Elisha, "Your servant my husband is dead, and you know that he revered the Lord. But now his creditor is coming to take my two boys as his slaves.*" (2 Kings 4:1).

Can you imagine how degrading, distressing and distracting this life of poverty and indebtedness must have been for this prophet and his family while he was alive and worse after his death? How does one concentrate on serving God wholeheartedly or delivering His messages effectively while being haunted by the threats and taunts of your creditors?

The gravity of the situation becomes even more obvious when you understand that debt in Hebrew culture was deeply stigmatized. To owe money meant you had failed to manage well—or that God hadn't blessed you!

How can a mother focus on fully serving God, while heavily burdened by the fear of losing her children – her immediate source of hope and consolation – to slavery and sorrow? How can children think of serving God when hunger pangs ravage their stomachs and their peers daily traumatize them with mocking looks and hurtful jibes – coupled with the realization that they may soon be torn from their mother and subjected to servitude?

The point here is that poverty, debt and financial stress often result in psychological (and sometimes physical) bondage and oppression. It is an established truth that "*the rich rule over the poor, and the borrower is slave to the lender*" (Proverbs 22:7). No wonder one of the covenant promises of God to His children is that "*The Lord will open the heavens, the storehouse of his bounty, to send rain on your land in season and to bless all the work of your hands. You will lend to many nations but will borrow from none*" (Deuteronomy 28:12).

May this be your portion in the name of Jesus!

3. Proof of God's faithfulness to His covenant

Take a look at Deuteronomy 8:18 (KJV) again – especially the last part: "*But thou shalt remember the LORD thy God: for it is he that giveth thee power to get wealth, that he may establish his covenant which he sware unto thy fathers, as it is this day.*"

What this affirms is that Kingdom prosperity is directly tied to the Abrahamic covenant, which includes not just spiritual blessings but also wealth, abundance and exponential increase. When believers prosper through God's principles, it confirms His faithfulness to His Word. Since God does not lie or make empty promises, when we fulfil our part by walking in obedience, prosperity becomes a visible validation of God's faithfulness across generations. It proves that the covenant is active in our lives.

4. Empowerment to fund Kingdom projects

The greatest purpose of Kingdom wealth is to drive God's work on earth. Prosperity in the hands of Kingdom-minded believers becomes a mighty tool for advancing the Gospel, supporting missions, planting and equipping churches, blessing workers and ministers in God's vineyard, translating and distributing Bibles, educating the next generation, and reaching out to the vulnerable through charity and humanitarian projects. Without such resources, many ministries would remain underfunded, their visions stalled, and their impact limited.

Throughout Scripture, we see how God strategically blessed His people with wealth to become financiers of His purposes. In the Old Testament, we read about King David, who, although not permitted to build the temple himself, amassed an enormous personal fortune to fund its construction. His words in 1 Chronicles 29:3 reveal his heart: *"In my devotion to the temple of my God I now give my personal treasures of gold and silver for the temple of my God, over and above everything I have provided for this holy temple."*

Similarly, in the New Testament, we saw earlier the remarkable example of the women and many others who supported Jesus' earthly ministry (Luke 8:2-3). Their resources enabled Jesus and His team to focus fully on the ministry without distraction or lack.

In the early church, a man named Barnabas also played a key role in supporting the burgeoning movement of the Gospel. Acts 4:36-37 records how he sold a field and laid the money at the apostles' feet, fueling the mission of the church in its critical, formative days. His act of generosity encouraged others, ensuring that no one among them suffered need.

Fast-forward to modern times, and the same pattern holds true. Behind every church building, charitable outreach, missionary journey, or every translated or freely distributed Bible, lies the unseen yet vital sacrifice of believers who understand that Kingdom wealth is not to be hoarded but to be invested. Their giving creates ripple effects that stretch beyond their lifetimes, often blessing people they will never meet.

Missionaries have been sent to the farthest reaches of the world because of Kingdom-minded givers. Churches have been planted in remote villages and urban centers alike because of the sacrificial generosity of believers. Organizations like Wycliffe Bible Translators, which focus on translating the Bible into every language, exist today because of consistent funding from Christians who understand that wealth is a tool for Kingdom advancement. Without such support, countless people would still be without access to God's Word in their native tongues.

Education too has been advanced by Kingdom wealth. Many of the world's leading universities were originally founded by Christian believers who sought to train ministers and advance learning in line with biblical values. Even today, Christian-owned schools and colleges across the globe operate through the funding and endowments of those who view their prosperity as a means of shaping future generations.

Likewise, humanitarian and charitable projects that reflect the love of Christ - feeding programs, hospitals, orphanages, disaster relief efforts - are largely funded by believers whose hearts are stirred to give. Countless church-based food pantries and clinics continue to impact millions through the faithful generosity of Christians who sow their resources into God's purposes.

This is the beauty and power of Kingdom prosperity; it turns financial resources into eternal fruit. The words of Paul to the Philippian church still ring true today: *"Not because I desire a gift: but I desire fruit that may abound to your account"* (Philippians 4:17). Through generous, faith-driven giving, believers store up treasure in heaven even as they expand God's Kingdom here on earth.

Indeed, without Kingdom-minded givers, many ministries would never reach their full potential. Their quiet sacrifices become the hidden streams that sustain mighty rivers of revival.

5. Opportunities to demonstrate generosity and love

Generosity is at the heart of Kingdom wealth. It moves the believer from a posture of need to a position of supply. When God prospers His children, He is not merely enriching us, He is enlisting us as living channels through which His compassion flows to a broken world. He is raising up distributors of mercy, ambassadors of generosity and investors in eternity.

Through Kingdom wealth, the believer becomes not just a receiver of blessing, but a vessel of it - pouring out love where the world expects only self-interest, and proving that Heaven's economy is one of grace, compassion, and limitless giving.

Someone rightly stated: "No one would remember the Good Samaritan if he only had good intentions, he had money as well." The more a believer prospers according to God's plan, the more capacity they have to extend mercy, alleviate suffering, and reflect the generous heart of the Father. Here is 2 Corinthians 9:8 (KJV) again: "*And God is able to make all grace abound toward you; that ye, always having all sufficiency in all things, may abound to every good work.*"

Many "good works" that bless lives in the church and community require good money. Prosperity enables believers to provide food for the hungry, cover the naked, rescue the abandoned, support the widow, and shelter the stranger. Without financial sufficiency, many righteous intentions remain unrealized. But when God prospers His children, He does so to equip us for righteous action.

James 2:14-15 emphasizes why the church needs prosperous believers: "*Suppose a brother or a sister is without clothes and daily food. If one of you says to them, "Go in peace; keep warm and well fed," but does nothing about their physical needs, what good is it?*"

Needy people, whether in the church or the community need more than kind or motivational words; genuine compassion requires action to help alleviate their suffering. This means providing practical assistance, such as food, clothing, or money when necessary. But how can this be possible if everyone believes poverty is the will of God?

Consider the example of the early church again. When wealthy believers sold their possessions and gave generously to meet the needs of others, the result was absolutely heartwarming! Acts 4:34 tells us: "*Neither was there any among them that lacked.*" This was a radical demonstration of love made possible through financial freedom. The Gospel advanced, hearts were encouraged, and needs were met. All because believers prospered and shared.

6. Testimony of God's goodness to the world

Sometimes, what truly convinces people that the gospel is good news is the visible manifestation of God's wonders in our lives. One of the ways God does this is by prospering His people.

Think about it: what kind of gospel can a Christian debtor preach to an unbelieving creditor, or to a landlord to whom he owes months or even years of rent - one that will sound believable? On the contrary, Kingdom wealth increases our capacity for impact by showcasing to the world that God cares for and blesses those who believe in Him.

The Lord Himself affirms that one major reason He showers covenant blessings upon His people is so that *"all the peoples on earth will see that you are called by the name of the Lord, and they will fear you"* (Deuteronomy 28:10). When the blessings of God are visibly evident in our lives, the gospel message becomes more tangible to unbelievers. It becomes easier for us to assure them that God is *"a rewarder of them that diligently seek Him."* (Hebrews 11:6). We can joyfully invite them into the Kingdom, just as Moses invited Hobab, his brother-in-law, saying: *"We are on our way to the place the Lord promised us, for He said, 'I will give it to you.' Come with us and we will treat you well, for the Lord has promised wonderful blessings for Israel!"* (Numbers 10:29, NLT).

In fact, Kingdom prosperity can draw people to the glory of God upon our lives, even without us saying a word. Isaiah 60:1–3 declares: *"Arise, shine, for your light has come, and the glory of the Lord rises upon you… Nations will come to your light, and kings to the brightness of your dawn."* Psalm 126:1–2 also proclaims: *"When the Lord restored the fortunes of Zion, we were like those who dreamed. Our mouths were filled with laughter, our tongues with songs of joy. Then it was said among the nations, 'The Lord has done great things for them.'"* I pray this will be your testimony too.

Moreover, Christ revealed that when we let the light of God within us shine before the world, and they see our good works - including acts of charity empowered by Kingdom prosperity - they will be moved to glorify our heavenly Father (Matthew 5:16). This is why Oral Roberts remarked, "Whoever controls the finances of a city or nation will control the spiritual climate as well."

The point is that wealth, when used rightly, can point people to God. Entrepreneurship, excellence, and economic influence become part of our Kingdom witness in society. Of course, prosperity isn't the gospel; but it can amplify it. As we fund scholarships, sponsor orphanages, pay hospital bills, or underwrite entire projects that transform communities and nations, the name of God is praised and the gospel breaks new frontiers.

7. **Breaking generational poverty and establishing legacy.**

Kingdom prosperity is generational in perspective. God desires that His blessings extend to future generations. Proverbs 13:22 (KJV) says: *"A good man leaveth an inheritance to his children's children."*

Kingdom wealth empowers us to leave financial legacies for our children and grandchildren, establish family foundations, scholarships, and charities, as well as create businesses that outlive us and continue advancing Kingdom causes This kind of wealth-building breaks cycles of poverty and creates generational blessings that extend far beyond one lifetime.

Ultimately, Kingdom wealth is never an end in itself. It is a powerful means of fulfilling God's purposes, blessing others, and securing eternal rewards through lasting legacies of faith, generosity, and righteousness.

PART 2

Fundamental Principles Of Kingdom Prosperity

4

TO REAP, YOU MUST SOW

"The Kingdom of God is a government with its own economy established through seedtime and harvest."

– Bill Winston

The law of sowing and reaping is the most fundamental principle established by God for the functioning of both the natural world and His eternal Kingdom. This means that if you can fully understand and consistently commit yourself to this law, you will have obtained the master key to victory and dominion in every area of your life, including your finances.

Although this principle has been active since the earliest period of human creation, it was after the flood - when Noah offered a sacrifice to God - that He made this solemn and decisive declaration: "*While the earth remaineth, seedtime and harvest, and cold and heat, and summer and winter, and day and night shall not cease*" (Genesis 8:22).

In this covenantal pronouncement, God permanently linked the principle of sowing and reaping to the rhythm of the earth and life itself. The implication is that just as day follows night and summer gives way to winter, every act of sowing leads to a harvest, whether in the natural or spiritual realm. Just as no one expects a harvest without planting, no one should expect increase or progress in any area of life without intentional investment.

This principle is so vital in God's Kingdom that Jesus embedded much of His teaching within it. On several occasions, He used sowing and reaping as metaphors to describe the operating system of the Kingdom. In fact, just after narrating the parable of the sower in Mark 4, He asked a pivotal question: "*Know ye not this parable? and how then will ye know all parables?*" (Mark 4:13, KJV).

What does this tell you? In the Kingdom, everything revolves around seed-sowing and harvest-reaping. Every decision we make, every act of service or neglect, every use of our time, talent, or resources is a seed; and every seed brings a harvest, sooner or later.

Paul reminded the Galatian church: "*Be not deceived; God is not mocked: for whatsoever a man soweth, that shall he also reap*" (Galatians 6:7).More importantly, Christ described

His own life and death as a seed that must be sown for the harvest of universal salvation to be realized. He said: "*Except a corn of wheat fall into the ground and die, it abideth alone: but if it die, it bringeth forth much fruit.*" (John 12:24)

By implication, no one is exempt from this divine law. Regardless of status, location, gender, race, nationality, profession, or religious affiliation - if you don't sow, you cannot reap. In fact, expecting to reap without sowing is a violation of divine order and leads to failure and sorrow. If you do not master and consciously apply this principle to your life, you will either continually struggle and serve others who sow, or be tempted to take shortcuts that can derail your life and destiny.

THE KINGDOM PROSPERITY ANGLE

Now, you may be wondering what this has to do with Kingdom prosperity. Let's revisit one of our key scriptures: "*But thou shalt remember the Lord thy God: for it is he that giveth thee power to get wealth…*" (Deuteronomy 8:18).

Notice that God does not bestow prosperity by simply dropping riches from the sky. Instead, He gives us the *power* to prosper. Power is the ability or capacity to do something. What God gives us, therefore, is the ability, wisdom, ideas, strength, connections, resources, opportunities, and above all, the favor we need to obtain wealth.

Each element of this power (with the exception of divine favor) is a seed. And just as a seed contains within it the potential for a harvest, so too does the power God gives us hold enormous possibilities for wealth, once His favor breathes upon it. This favor is extremely important because it is what catalyzes our seed to produce such supernatural abundance that far exceeds what the world can achieve through natural means.

WHAT IT MEANS TO SOW – MAXIMIZING YOUR POWER FOR KINGDOM WEALTH

One thing is clear from both scriptural and contemporary evidence: every Kingdom-prospered person is a committed and consistent sower. They never tire of investing their time, energy, talents, skills, finances, and other resources in purposeful and strategic ways. And the Lord blesses their investments with His wealth-galvanizing favor.

Take the example of Isaac. How was Kingdom wealth activated in his life? Was it simply because he was Abraham's son? Not at all. "*Then Isaac sowed in that land, and received in the same year a hundredfold: and the Lord blessed him.*" (Genesis 26:12). Did you see the sequence? Isaac recognized the power he had -his seeds and strength - and sowed it despite prevailing scarcity. Then the Lord blessed him.

Consider also the widow whose prophet-husband died in debt. As destitute as she believed herself to be, Elisha made it clear that her financial breakthrough would not magically fall from heaven. Instead, it would come from identifying the power for wealth that God had already given her and "sowing" or maximizing it.

"Elisha replied to her, 'How can I help you? Tell me, what do you have in your house?' 'Your servant has nothing there at all,' she said, 'except a small jar of olive oil.' Elisha said, 'Go around and ask all your neighbors for empty jars. Don't ask for just a few. Then go inside and shut the door behind you and your sons. Pour oil into all the jars, and as each is filled, put it to one side.' She left him and shut the door behind her and her sons. They brought the jars to her and she kept pouring. When all the jars were full, she said to her son, 'Bring me another one.' But he replied, 'There is not a jar left.' Then the oil stopped flowing. She went and told the man of God, and he said, 'Go, sell the oil and pay your debts. You and your sons can live on what is left." 2 Kings 4:2–7)

Did you see the various seeds sown by this woman who thought she had nothing? She sowed her resource - the olive oil she kept pouring. She sowed her energy - going around to collect jars and filling them until there were none left. And she had clearly invested in her relationships, which is why her neighbors willingly gave her the jars she needed. And as she sowed, God Almighty delivered her from debt and lack.

When Christ too needed money to pay the temple for Himself and Peter, He didn't call down money from heaven. Instead, He told Peter to deploy his fishing skill; and through that act of obedience, Peter received a divine harvest.

So, how does all this apply to you? Let me give you a detailed and practical breakdown.

SOWING YOUR TIME

Time is one of the most powerful seeds God has given to each of us - in equal measure, but not with the same outcome. Whether rich or poor, young or old, educated or uneducated, we all wake up each day with the same 24 hours. Yet, the results those hours produce vary widely from one person to another. What sets people apart, especially those who build wealth and influence, is how they invest those hours. In other words, prosperity is not just about how much you do, but how intentionally you use your time to serve and create value.

As a believer, time must never be regarded as something to spend carelessly, but as a divine seed meant for intentional sowing. Ephesians 5:15–16 exhorts us to "*walk circumspectly, not as fools, but as wise, redeeming the time, because the days are evil.*"

"Redeeming" implies buying something back or recovering what is slipping away. Redeeming time therefore means buying it back from misuse, waste, and distraction – that is, treating each minute as an investment into seeking and fulfilling your God-given purpose. It means ordering your days with a sense of purpose and urgency. Psalm 90:12 says, *"So teach us to number our days, that we may apply our hearts unto wisdom."*

Believers who desire Kingdom prosperity don't just "spend" time; they invest it strategically. As Dr. Munroe once said, "The currency of life is time, not money. Waste your time and you've wasted your life." This is why wise people throughout history have always made time management a non-negotiable priority.

Financial blessings are often delayed not because God isn't willing, but because many are not sowing their time with purpose. I find it ridiculous how people can complain about a lack of opportunities or finances, while spending hours binge-watching television shows, scrolling endlessly through social media, engaging in group chats and gossips that never end, or waiting passively for "breakthrough.". You cannot complain about lack and then waste time daily. Financial prosperity comes to those who are faithful with their time before they are trusted with treasure.

One technique that can help you is the Pareto Principle, also called the 80/20 rule. It says that roughly 80 percent of your results come from 20 percent of your efforts. So instead of trying to do everything, identify the few high-impact activities that give you the biggest return and focus your energy there. Not everything that screams for your attention deserves your time. Learn to distinguish between what is urgent and what is important. The secret is to ask, "What few things today will really move me toward my purpose?" Then structure your time around those. Plan your day the night before. Block time for what matters. Track how you spend your hours for a few days; it may surprise you how much time slips away unnoticed. Once you see the pattern, you can start to redeem it.

I once read an interesting illustration that will sharpen your time investment instinct. Imagine that each day, you receive $1,440 into your account with the condition that anything you don't use by the end of the day disappears. What would you do? You would use every cent to your advantage. That's exactly how time works: you are credited with 1,440 minutes each day. Whatever you fail to invest in the fulfilment of God's purpose and the development of your potential is lost forever. It cannot be rolled over, and it cannot be retrieved.

This understanding should compel you to structure your day with intentionality. Set daily goals that align with your vision. Prioritize high-value tasks that move you closer to your God-ordained destiny. This means allocating quality time for communion with God, creativity, productivity, and rest. Read books on wealth creation from Christian and ethical perspectives. Enroll in trainings that sharpen your financial literacy, leadership, or entrepreneurial skill. Spend time planning your budget, evaluating your habits, and setting clear financial goals.

You must keep asking yourself: *Where is my time going? How am I using it to create value for God's kingdom, for myself and for humanity?* Let that spur you daily to treat your time like you would your money. Budget it. Invest it. Protect it. Because when you sow it wisely, especially toward the things God expects of you, He will release uncommon favor on your effort.

SOWING YOUR SKILLS, TALENTS, AND IDEAS

Every believer carries within him or her a unique and powerful deposit from God. It may not always look significant at first, but it is a seed with the potential to unlock doors, generate income, solve problems, and fund Kingdom advancement. These deposits often come in the form of gifts, skills, talents and creative ideas. And just like the farmer must sow seed to expect a harvest, believers must learn to identify, sharpen, and invest their talents to reap Kingdom prosperity.

Jesus told the parable of the talents in Matthew 25:14–30, where three servants were entrusted with resources according to their ability. The two who invested and multiplied what they were given were rewarded and promoted. The one who buried his talent, perhaps out of fear, laziness or discontent, was rebuked and stripped of even what he had. The lesson here is that God's Kingdom rewards productivity. Talents must not be buried in excuses or hidden behind spirituality. They must be sown for Kingdom use and for the benefit of humanity.

The Scripture reveals that "*a man's gift makes room for him, and brings him before great men*" (Proverbs 18:16). How did David, an overlooked shepherd boy first found his way into the palace? Not by killing Goliath but by developing and deploying his musical skills, which impressed those who heard him and got him recommended to Saul, the king (1 Samuel 16).

Indeed, the Bible is full of such individuals who prospered by harnessing and maximizing what God had deposited in them. Joseph had the gift of administration and interpretation of dreams. In prison, he didn't let those gifts lie dormant. He used them to help others, and eventually, those same gifts opened the doors of Pharaoh's palace and positioned him as a ruler over Egypt. He didn't need money to rise; he sowed his skill, and God multiplied the harvest.

In Exodus 31:1–5, God tells Moses that He has filled Bezalel with the Spirit of God in wisdom, understanding, and knowledge to create artistic works for the tabernacle. Likewise, your gifts and skills - whether in design, speaking, coding, teaching, writing, organizing, building, strategizing, or selling - are Kingdom seeds. When they are left unsharpened or unused, the potential harvest is lost.

Sowing your skills begins with discovery. Many people underestimate themselves because they've never taken the time to evaluate what they do well. Sometimes, your skill may be so natural to you that you don't even recognize it as valuable. But every talent has marketable worth when refined and aligned with purpose. Ask yourself: *What do I do with ease that others find difficult? What do people usually commend me for? What problem am I passionate about solving?* That may lead you to the "seed" of your talent or calling.

After discovery comes development. No matter how gifted you are, an undeveloped talent will never command attention or generate wealth. Proverbs 22:29 asks, *"Seest thou a man diligent in his business? he shall stand before kings; he shall not stand before mean men."* Skill is sharpened through training, mentoring, practice, feedback, and exposure. Even David, before he defeated Goliath, had honed his sling in the field while tending sheep. Don't be content with raw potential; process it into something valuable and marketable.

Then comes deployment. Prosperity doesn't flow from unused ability. You must find a platform for expression. Serve God and others with your gift. Offer your skill to your church, workplace, community, or online marketplace. Create solutions. Solve problems. Add value. When your skill begins to meet needs, people will begin to seek you out and reward you.

Finally, there is monetization. This is where your skills begin to translate into resources. And here again is where you must be wise as a believer. There is nothing unspiritual about earning from your God-given gift. If the world pays for knowledge, ideas, and skill, why should the believer's gift be locked in poverty? Monetizing your skill simply means creating value in such a way that others are willing to pay for it, whether through products, services, consultancy, business, or entrepreneurship.

So, ask yourself: What do I carry that I've not yet sown? What can I learn to do better? What idea am I sitting on that needs attention? Start sowing. Start refining. Start sharing. Your prosperity may be locked inside the very thing you've been ignoring!

SOWING FINANCIAL RESOURCES

Just as a farmer cannot expect a harvest from a field he has never planted, no believer can flourish in Kingdom prosperity without engaging the principle of financial sowing. No matter how hard you think things are for you, you are not exempted from financial sowing. This is why Jesus recognized and commended the poor widow who offered all she had to God (Mark 12:41–44). He could have discouraged her from giving, considering her condition but He perfectly understood the law of sowing and reaping and was certain that the woman would be abundantly rewarded by God. As the Scripture says, *"Whoever sows sparingly will also reap sparingly, and whoever sows generously will also reap generously. Each of you should give what you have decided in your heart to give, not reluctantly or under compulsion, for God loves a cheerful giver."* (2 Corinthians 9:6-7).

There are many ways believers can sow financially, and each is a pathway to Kingdom expansion and divine blessings. Whether you're tithing faithfully, giving to missions, helping someone in need, investing in a business idea, or saving toward a godly goal, you're planting financial seeds that will bear fruit in this life and beyond. We will explore the details in subsequent chapters.

SOWING INTO RELATIONSHIPS AND NETWORKS

This is a critical Kingdom principle that many overlook. While attention often centers on giving money, time, or skills, the truth is that God often channels His blessings to us through people. Doors don't usually open by themselves; someone, somewhere, pulls the handle. The favor that unlocks the next level in your life may be tied to someone you've served, honored, helped, or simply related with in integrity and love.

Proverbs 18:24 says, *"A man that hath friends must show himself friendly..."*—and we might add: a man who wants to prosper must sow into the right relationships. This doesn't mean building connections for selfish reasons. It means learning to value the people God places in your life as stewards of opportunity, wisdom, and increase. David ascended the throne through Jonathan's loyalty and Samuel's endorsement. Ruth's future changed dramatically because she stayed connected to Naomi. Elisha stepped into double-portion anointing because he stayed faithfully connected to Elijah. Joseph's name was mentioned in Pharaoh's ears because of the relationship he had with the king's butler. In every case, relational loyalty opened the door to divine elevation.

In today's world, this means being intentional about the people you associate with. It means humbling yourself to serve a mentor, learning from those ahead of you, and not isolating yourself in pride or independence. Proverbs 27:17 says, *"Iron sharpeneth iron; so a man sharpeneth the countenance of his friend."* Relationships can stretch you, refine your thinking, expand your worldview, and challenge you to grow into the fullness of your calling.

But relationships are not only about what you can get; they are also fertile ground to sow trust, kindness, encouragement, and help. Being present in someone's low moment, offering a word of wisdom or a helping hand, can be the seed that produces a future harvest of support when you need it most. Galatians 6:10

encourages us: *"As we have therefore opportunity, let us do good unto all men, especially unto them who are of the household of faith."*

SOWING EFFORT AND PERSISTENCE

Kingdom prosperity does not respond to laziness. No matter how many prophetic declarations are spoken over your life, or how great your potential is, if you do not rise up with energy and persist through the process, you will remain stuck in a cycle of frustration. Proverbs 10:4 (KJV) says it plainly: *"He becometh poor that dealeth with a slack hand: but the hand of the diligent maketh rich."* Prosperity is never attracted to passivity. It flows toward focused, consistent, determined action.

Diligence is so fundamental to prosperity that its absence can cause even someone born into wealth, or someone with massive potential for success, to end up in poverty and misery. Proverbs 24:30–34 illustrates this clearly: "*I walked by the field of a lazy person, the vineyard of one with no common sense. I saw that it was overgrown with nettles. It was covered with weeds, and its walls were broken down. Then, as I looked and thought about it, I learned this lesson: A little extra sleep, a little more slumber, a little folding of the hands to rest— then poverty will pounce on you like a bandit; scarcity will attack you like an armed robber.*"

Do you see how tragic that man's situation was? He already had a vineyard, either inherited or planted for him. All he needed to do was invest the effort to maintain and develop what he had. But laziness and overindulgence ruined him.

Note that laziness isn't just about lying in bed all day. It often shows up in more subtle, socially acceptable ways, such as procrastination, inconsistency, blaming others, waiting for perfect conditions, and endlessly "planning" without executing. Ecclesiastes 11:4 warns: "*He that observeth the wind shall not sow; and he that regardeth the clouds shall not reap.*" In other words, if you keep waiting for ideal circumstances, you'll never take action. And without sowing, there can be no harvest.

Every vision requires motion, and every purpose demands effort. You must wake up with intention, work with a passion for excellence, and press forward with focus. Even when results are slow, diligence is the key that keeps your engine running.

Consider Isaac in Genesis 26. He faced adversity when the Philistines stopped up the wells his father had dug. But instead of quitting or cursing his opposition, Isaac rolled up his sleeves and kept digging. He dug again, and the enemy contended with him. He dug yet another and still faced contention. But he didn't stop.

Finally, he dug a well, and there was no strife. He named it Rehoboth, saying: "*For now the Lord hath made room for us, and we shall be fruitful in the land*" (Genesis 26:22, KJV)

That is the spirit of persistence. Many believers dig once or twice and give up when resistance shows up. But resistance is part of the process. Delays and disappointments don't mean God has denied you; they may simply mean He is working on the seeds you are sowing. A lazy hand interprets challenges as a sign to stop. But true sowers take steps of faith. They show up, work hard, plan carefully, and persist when others quit. Over time, this steady faithfulness produces lasting prosperity.

Your Rehoboth of abundance is on the other side of your diligent and persistent sowing.

5

PRIORITIZE GOD'S KINGDOM, NOT MAMMON

"There is nothing wrong with men possessing riches. The wrong comes when riches possess men."

- Billy Graham

Kingdom wealth is activated when we make the Kingdom, and not wealth, our priority. This is one of the profound paradoxes of God's Kingdom and a powerful pivot point for understanding Kingdom prosperity. A divine paradox is a truth that seems contradictory by human standards but reveals deep spiritual wisdom. That's what we aim to unravel in this chapter; and even though you may find some of the revelations jolting, they are essential if what you truly desire is the blessing of God that makes rich and adds no sorrow.

While we've emphasized the necessity of sowing in the previous chapter, it's important to understand that the ultimate result of your sowing is not entirely within your control. Of course, sowing is absolutely necessary, since God Himself demands it; but it is not the sowing alone that produces the final outcome. God is the one who determines and bestows the harvest. In doing so, He considers not only our sowing efforts but also His purpose for our lives and our capacity to manage what He gives. That capacity involves faithfulness, discipline and wisdom.

This is why it's called *Kingdom wealth*, not *worldly wealth*. And this is why we are stewards, not owners. As previously noted, Kingdom wealth is not about having riches for their own sake, but about wealth tied to purpose and capacity. Therefore, even as we sow continually, God oversees our harvest according to His wisdom. Jesus illustrated this in Matthew 25:14–15: "*Again, it will be like a man going on a journey, who called his servants and entrusted his wealth to them. To one he gave five bags of gold, to another two bags, and to another one bag, each according to his ability…*"

That's exactly how God releases Kingdom wealth - according to our ability to steward it. The reason for this is implied in Matthew 7:9–10: "*Which of you, if your son asks for bread, will give him a stone? Or if he asks for a fish, will give him a snake?*"

God is as much our protector as He is our provider. Entrusting wealth without regard for purpose and capacity is like giving a stone or a serpent to a child; it would break the child's teeth or poison their system.

Wealth that is not attached to purpose and capacity often leads to impulsive spending, broken relationships, and emotional instability. We see this frequently in the lives of those who stumble into worldly wealth. Many lottery winners, for example, end up bankrupt and estranged from family within a few years. In contrast, Kingdom wealth is wisely apportioned by God so that what is meant to bless us does not become a curse. Here is Dr Munroe again: "God does not give us too much or too little. He gives us just enough to fulfil our purpose."

IT'S ALL ABOUT GOD

Let's make this even easier to grasp. Take your mind off Kingdom wealth for a moment and consider another blessing - long life. While it's true that God has promised us a long and healthy life, He is ultimately the one who determines how long each of us lives. As Job 14:5 affirms: "*A person's days are determined; you have decreed the number of his months and have set limits he cannot exceed.*"

But does this mean we shouldn't sow into our health by taking care of ourselves, eating well, maintaining hygiene, living a healthy lifestyle, and taking safety precautions? Of course not. We do all that we can, while remaining conscious that the length of our days is ultimately in God's hands.

This is how Kingdom prosperity operates as well. We sow faithfully and diligently, but with the understanding that the level of increase or prosperity each person receives is in God's hands. As Mark 4:26–29 explains: "*…A man scatters seed on the ground. Night and day, whether he sleeps or gets up, the seed sprouts and grows, though he does not know how. All by itself the soil produces grain—first the stalk, then the head, then the full kernel in the head. As soon as the grain is ripe, he puts the sickle to it, because the harvest has come.*" Apostle Paul puts it even more bluntly in his letter to the Corinthians: "*I planted, Apollos watered, but God gave the increase. So then neither he who plants is anything, nor he who waters, but God who gives the increase.*" (1 Corinthians 3:6–7, NKJV)

PROSPERITY IMPLICATIONS

There are six key implications of the truth that God plays a sovereign role over every aspect of our lives, including Kingdom prosperity.

1. **Kingdom prosperity is not received through desperation**

Proverbs 23:4 gives a strict warning: "*Do not overwork to be rich…*" (NKJV). When we understand that all our sowing and toiling in the Kingdom are simply what is expected of us (Luke 17:10), and that the ultimate reward comes from God Himself, we are freed from desperation. We do not jeopardize our souls or compromise our Kingdom commitments in pursuit of wealth. While financial literacy, diligent labor, and a passion for excellence are important, we must not allow the pursuit of money to become idolatrous, thereby mortgaging our eternal destiny for material gain. "*For what will it profit a man if he gains the whole world, and loses his own soul?*" (Mark 8:36, NKJV).

This understanding helps us maintain the right perspective and keep our priorities aligned as we await our harvest of blessings. Kingdom wealth is a *byproduct* of Kingdom living. Therefore, we must not ignore the substance while chasing its shadow. Jesus said: "*So do not worry, saying, 'What shall we eat?' or 'What shall we drink?' or 'What shall we wear?' For the pagans run after all these things, and your heavenly Father knows that you need them. But seek first his kingdom and his righteousness, and all these things will be given to you as well.*" *(Matthew 6:31–33)*

The people of the world center their lives on wealth accumulation because they are governed by natural laws and have no hope beyond this life. Their outcomes are strictly determined by their input. But the believer's life is supernatural – that is, connected to the natural world, yet not confined by it. Divine grace guarantees exponential increase beyond what our efforts alone could produce.

Moreover, as strangers and pilgrims on earth, our hopes extend far beyond this realm. Therefore, we do not pursue wealth the way the world does. We do not neglect our spiritual life, ministry, family, or physical well-being in the quest for riches. God's Word is categorical: "*But people who long to be rich fall into temptation and are trapped by many foolish and harmful desires that plunge them into ruin and destruction. For the love of money is the root of all kinds of evil. And some people, craving money, have wandered from the true faith and pierced themselves with many sorrows.*" *(1 Timothy 6:9–10, NLT)*

The Amplified Bible puts it this way: "*Those who [are not financially ethical and] crave to get rich [with a compulsive, greedy longing for wealth] fall into temptation and a trap and into many foolish and harmful desires that plunge people into ruin and destruction [leading to personal misery]. For the love of money [that is, the greedy desire for it and the willingness to gain it unethically] is a root of all sorts of evil, and some by longing for it have wandered away from the faith and pierced themselves [through and through] with many sorrows.*"

It is indeed saddening to see believers driven by desperation for money to the point of becoming lukewarm toward the things of God. Some take jobs that compromise their faith or fall into financial traps that promise quick wealth but deliver deep regret. These include Ponzi schemes, money-doubling scams, gambling, betting, and other dubious entanglements. Others are caught embezzling funds, collecting kickbacks, inflating costs, or committing outright fraud.

Such desperation damages faith, reputation, and relationships, and often leaves behind nothing but emptiness. We must not be pressured by what we see or feel around us. The understanding that God's dealings and timing differ for each individual should keep us from anxiety, envy, or unhealthy competition.

Consider those who were blessed with Kingdom prosperity in Scripture; it was never through obsession with wealth. When Abraham was called by God and he obeyed, his primary focus was pleasing God. Yet God blessed Him abundantly. What about Isaac? He simply listened to God at a time of famine and took a step of faith. Desperation could have pushed him to move elsewhere but because his spirit remained attuned to Heaven's frequency, he was able to receive the Word that forbade him from leaving and his blessing came eventually.

The case of Solomon was particularly striking. He became wealthy because his primary concern was pleasing God and leading His people aright, so much that even when God gave him the opportunity to make a request, all he asked for was divine presence and guidance. This was why God prospered him, even without his direct request. "*So God said to him, "Since you have asked for this and not for long life or wealth for yourself, nor have asked for the death of your enemies but for discernment in administering justice, I will do what you have asked. I will give you a wise and discerning heart, so that there will never have been anyone like you, nor will there ever be. Moreover, I will give you what you have not asked for—both wealth and honor —so that in your lifetime you will have no equal among kings*" (1 Kings 3:11-13).

This is how prosperity flows in the Kingdom. Jesus didn't mince words: "*No one can serve two masters. Either you will hate the one and love the other, or you will be devoted to the one and despise the other. You cannot serve both God and money*" (Matthew 6:24). He also declared: "'*Love the Lord your God with all your heart and with all your soul and with all your mind.' This is the first and greatest commandment*" *(Matthew 22:37–38).*

That is the divine safeguard against desperation. Even when we give to God and others, our primary motivation must be love and devotion to God, not merely the expectation of return. Love for God and His Kingdom must come first, not love for His blessings.

Otherwise, we risk falling into the trap of transactional faith, treating God like a vending machine and becoming frustrated when He proves He is not one.

2. Prosperity is not preserved by obsession

Just as Kingdom prosperity is not obtained through desperation, it is not preserved through obsession. This is a mistake many people make, and one you must avoid. Shifting your focus from God, the Giver, to the preservation or multiplication of the blessing itself can lead to the loss of both the blessing and your soul.

This was the error of the rich fool in Jesus' parable: "*The ground of a certain rich man yielded an abundant harvest. He thought to himself, 'What shall I do? I have no place to store my crops.' Then he said, 'This is what I'll do. I will tear down my barns and build bigger ones, and there I will store my surplus grain. And I'll say to myself, "You have plenty of grain laid up for many years. Take life easy; eat, drink and be merry."' But God said to him, 'You fool! This very night your life will be demanded from you. Then who will get what you have prepared for yourself?' This is how it will be with whoever stores up things for themselves but is not rich toward God*" (Luke 12:16–21).

After being blessed, all that occupied the man's mind was how to preserve the blessing for himself. Notice how many times he used "I", but not once did he mention "God." He had relegated God to the background while obsessing over his wealth. Those who understand Kingdom wealth know this is not the way to keep it flowing.

Now, compare the rich fool's attitude with that of Abraham. One reason Abraham continued to be blessed was that he acknowledged God as the source of all he had. Not only did he build altars of worship wherever he went, but he also remained calm and unshaken about his wealth. A clear example is his encounter with Lot. When they were about to separate, Abraham, though the elder and the one through whom Lot had been blessed, allowed Lot to choose any part of the land he preferred. Abraham was confident that wherever Lot left for him would be blessed, because his connection to God was intact. He understood that the blessing was not merely the result of his labor, but a product of God's mercy.

And God proved him right: "*The Lord said to Abram after Lot had parted from him, 'Look around from where you are, to the north and south, to the east and west. All the land that you see I will give to you and your offspring forever. I will make your offspring like the dust of the earth… Go, walk through the length and breadth of the land, for I am giving it to you.' So Abram went to live near the great trees of Mamre at Hebron, where he pitched his tents. There he built an altar to the Lord*" (Genesis 13:14–18).

No matter how many competitors you have in your line of business, don't become anxious or agitated by what they're doing that you forget God. If you remain calm and consistently acknowledge God like Abraham did, He will always give you an edge.

3. Prosperity does not equate to spirituality

As we've seen, prosperity is apportioned to diligent sowers based on God's purpose for their lives and their capacity to manage it. It is not a measure of spiritual condition. Therefore, a higher level of prosperity does not automatically mean a higher level of spirituality.

This is important to emphasize because it's easy to be lulled into spiritual slumber by the deceitfulness of riches - thinking that material success means all is well spiritually, even when we're drifting away. Such thinking can hinder the flow of divine prosperity altogether.

The Laodicean church is a prime example. Located in a city renowned for its economic prosperity, they became wealthy and misinterpreted their wealth as a sign of spiritual health. They became complacent, self-sufficient, and lukewarm in faith, failing to examine themselves. This earned them a sharp rebuke from the Giver: "*You say, 'I am rich; I have acquired wealth and do not need a thing.' But you do not realize that you are wretched, pitiful, poor, blind and naked. I counsel you to buy from me gold refined in the fire, so you can become rich; and white clothes to wear, so you can cover your shameful nakedness; and salve to put on your eyes, so you can see. Those whom I love I rebuke and discipline. So be earnest and repent.*" (Revelation 3:17–19).

May you never find yourself in such a dreadful situation.

4. Prosperity should not define your existence or happiness

Christ gives a stern warning in Luke 12:15: "*Watch out! Be on your guard against all kinds of greed; life does not consist in an abundance of possessions.*"

Knowing that God is the Giver and Owner of Kingdom prosperity, it is unwise to build our existence or happiness around it. Our lives must be so anchored in God that our daily joy flows from Him, not from our bank accounts. As

Allowing the state of our finances to determine our state of mind is not only a recipe for idolatry and stinginess, but also a gateway to anxiety and frustration. Proverbs 23:5 reminds us: "*For riches certainly make themselves wings; they fly away like an eagle toward heaven.*"

Some people tie their entire identity to their wealth, so much so that their moods and even blood pressure fluctuate with financial gains or losses. For them, the loss of wealth makes life feel meaningless, and tragically, some even resort to suicide. A study across 36 countries found that suicide rates increased during years of significant stock market decline and the year following it. During the 2008 financial crisis, an estimated 6,566 additional suicides occurred globally as a direct consequence of the crash.

This is not the mindset of those who understand Kingdom wealth. In Matthew 19:20–22 (KJV), Jesus reveals the mentality required to handle Kingdom wealth: "*The young man said to Him, 'All these things I have kept from my youth. What do I still lack?' Jesus said to him, 'If you want to be perfect, go, sell what you have and give to the poor, and you will have treasure in heaven; and come, follow Me.' But when the young man heard that saying, he went away sorrowful, for he had great possessions.*"

Christ made it clear that in the Kingdom, wealth is not about status but about purpose. But for a man who had woven his identity around his possessions, that truth was too difficult to accept.

Now compare that man with Job, who after losing everything declared: "*Naked I came from my mother's womb, and naked I will depart. The LORD gave and the LORD has taken away; may the name of the LORD be praised*" (Job 1:21). That was a man who understood the dynamics of Kingdom wealth. No wonder God doubled all he lost.

The same was true of Abraham. After waiting years for a child, he didn't make his world revolve around Isaac. When God asked for Isaac as a sacrifice, Abraham didn't hesitate. Why? Because despite the blessing, his heart remained fully devoted to the Giver. God's response was powerful: "*I swear by myself, declares the LORD, that because you have done this and have not withheld your son, your only son, I will surely bless you and make your descendants as numerous as the stars in the sky and as the sand on the seashore. Your descendants will take possession of the cities of their enemies, and through your offspring all nations on earth will be blessed, because you have obeyed me*" (Genesis 22:16–18)

So, if you want Kingdom wealth to be continually released and increased in your life, then don't center your life around it.

5. Prosperity should not cause pride or snobbery

1 Corinthians 4:7 asks a thought-provoking question: "*For who makes you different from anyone else? What do you have that you did not receive? And if you did receive it, why do you boast as though you did not?*"

Since God is the one who activates and apportions prosperity, the right attitude that keeps heaven open to us is thankfulness and humility. Yes, you may be smart and hardworking; but both the power and the favor to get wealth come from God, not merely from your labor.

There are many people who are even more brilliant and hardworking than you, yet they do not possess the same level of wealth.

Ecclesiastes 9:11 affirms this: "*I have seen something else under the sun: The race is not to the swift or the battle to the strong, nor does food come to the wise or wealth to the brilliant or favor to the learned; but time and chance happen to them all.*"

This should constantly remind you that your wealth does not make you better, superior, or part of a higher "class" than others. It's all by the mercies of God. This understanding should keep you ever grateful to God and considerate of others. As Paul instructed: "*Command those who are rich in this present world not to be arrogant nor to put their hope in wealth, which is so uncertain, but to put their hope in God, who richly provides us with everything for our enjoyment*" (1 Timothy 6:17).

This posture of humility ensures continued favor and lifting from above: "*For those who exalt themselves will be humbled, and those who humble themselves will be exalted*" (Matthew 23:12),

6. Prosperity grows through generosity, not stinginess

This is another interesting paradox about Kingdom wealth. It doesn't grow by being locked away; it multiplies when it's released. In the natural world, people often believe that hoarding wealth secures it. But in the Kingdom of God, the opposite is true. The more you clutch it tightly, the more it slips through your fingers. The more you sow it into God's purposes, the more it flourishes.

Proverbs 11:24 (NKJV) says it plainly: "*There is one who scatters, yet increases more; And there is one who withholds more than is right, But it leads to poverty.*" Notice the nuance here. Scripture acknowledges that some withholding is "right"; in other words, there's wisdom in saving, planning, and managing resources well. But it draws a clear line between wise stewardship and selfish stinginess. When we cross into the territory of hoarding out of fear or greed, we don't preserve wealth; we poison it. What was meant to be a blessing begins to decay.

This principle may seem counterintuitive, but it's the rhythm of Kingdom economics. Proverbs 11:25 (KJV) reinforces it: "*The liberal soul shall be made fat: and he that watereth shall be watered also himself.*" God doesn't just reward giving; He multiplies it. Why? Because generosity reveals the heart of a faithful steward. When we give freely, we show that we understand wealth is not ours to possess, but ours to distribute. We become conduits, not containers.

Kingdom prosperity isn't about accumulation—it's about circulation. It flows through us, not just to us. And the more we align our resources with God's purposes by supporting God's work, helping the needy, building the church, and uplifting others, the more He entrusts to us. So let's not fall into the trap of scarcity thinking. Stinginess may feel safe, but it leads to spiritual and financial drought. Generosity, on the other hand, opens the floodgates of divine provision. In the Kingdom, giving is not subtraction; it's multiplication.

Let us see the diverse ways we can actualize this Kingdom multiplication in the next chapter.

6

ENGAGE IN COVENANT GIVING FOR GENERATIONAL PROSPERITY

"When you plant your seed in the Kingdom of God, the Lord will multiply it far better than Wall Street."

- John Hagee

We saw in the previous chapter that Kingdom prosperity is not merely based on our diligence, stewardship and sowing but also our purpose and capacity. A major determinant of this capacity is the depth of our obedience and faithfulness in Kingdom matters, especially covenant giving.

Covenant giving is giving that goes beyond the casual to the intentional, from the general to the sacrificial. It is giving that goes beyond what you can spare but what

God commands and what your heart willingly obeys and releases. It is the kind of giving that moves God, not because of the size, but because of the honour, faith, and sacrifice behind it. This is what Hebrews 11:4 (NKJV) refers to, when it says, "*By faith Abel offered to God a more excellent sacrifice than Cain, through which he obtained witness that he was righteous, God testifying of his gifts…*" It was the kind of giving David meant when he said, "*I will not sacrifice to the LORD my God burnt offerings that cost me nothing*" (2 Samuel 24:24).

Covenant, by nature, is a binding promise sealed with mutual responsibility. Therefore, when we engage in covenant giving, we are not tipping God; we are entering into a sacred arrangement where our obedience provokes Heaven's commitment to bless and defend us. In other words, when you engage in covenant giving, you are not merely giving to God; you are engaging a divine protocol that enlists heaven's partnership in your prosperity journey. You are building eternal equity in God's economy. That's a solid investment that not only guarantees abundant profitability but is imbued with failproof security. "*Store your treasures in heaven, where moths and rust cannot destroy, and thieves do not break in and steal*" (Matthew 6:19-20, NLT)

By implication, covenant giving doesn't just meet your needs. It activates *Kingdom surplus* and positions you to be a blessing to others. The blessings of covenant giving are not limited to finances. They extend to health, family, divine ideas, divine ideas, favor, stability, and generational wealth. Abraham's covenant with God made him not just rich but transgenerationally prosperous. *"In blessing I will bless thee… and thy seed shall possess the gate of his enemies"* (Genesis 22:17, KJV).

Understand also that covenant giving is not a transactional scheme in the worldly sense. It is not about manipulating God but partnering with Him and trusting that He is faithful to do what He has promised. In this partnership, your giving serves as an act of worship that ties your resources to God's unfailing covenant, unleashing a cycle of provision that reaches beyond personal gain into generational impact.

Essentially, covenant giving is special because:

- **It is relational, not transactional.** You give as one in covenant-relationship with God, not as a customer seeking divine services.
- **It is obedience-driven, not emotionally driven.** It flows from the revelation of Scripture, not from the hype of a moment.
- **It is backed by divine accountability.** God, who initiated the covenant, is bound to honor His promises when you honor your part. In other words, Covenant giving is giving that God cannot ignore.

FORMS OF COVENANT GIVING

Covenant giving is based on key biblical practices that establish and maintain the flow of Kingdom wealth. These include:

1. Tithing

Tithing is a sacred act of returning to God the first tenth of all our income. It is not merely a financial transaction, but a spiritual declaration that God is our ultimate source and owner of everything we possess. When we tithe, we are not giving to God; we are returning what already belongs to Him. This act of obedience and honor sanctifies the remainder of our resources, placing our finances under divine order and blessing.

In Malachi 3:10–12, God outlines the covenant promise tied to tithing. "*Bring ye all the tithes into the storehouse, that there may be meat in mine house, and prove me now herewith, saith the LORD of hosts, if I will not open you the windows of heaven, and pour you out a blessing, that there shall not be room enough to receive it. And I will rebuke the devourer for your sakes, and he shall not destroy the fruits of your ground; neither shall your vine cast her fruit before the time in the field, saith the LORD of hosts. And all nations shall call you blessed: for ye shall be a delightsome land, saith the LORD of hosts*" (Malachi 3:10-12).

This is the only place in Scripture where God invites us to test Him and this should tell you how important tithing is in the Kingdom. Tithing activates divine protection over your finances. Many believers work hard, yet their resources are consumed by illness, crisis, and debt. Without the tithe, the devourer has legal access. But when you tithe, God becomes your financial defender. It is like a spiritual insurance policy that secures your field and sustains your fruit. The tithe places your finances under covenant covering, where divine favor and supernatural provision flow.

In essence, when you tithe, you enjoy open heavens, with resources, revelations, and divine help flowing freely to you; you escape financial curses, with your life becoming a landing ground for blessing; you triumph over every devourer; your life becomes a testimony as "all nations shall call you blessed" and you emerge as a delightsome wonder, with people wanting to be around you, partnering with you, investing in you.

Note that tithing is not limited to one era or generation. It is trans-dispensational and trans-generational. Abraham tithed to Melchizedek long before the Law was given, recognizing God's hand in his victory (Genesis 14:18-20). Jacob vowed to tithe as part of his covenant with God, pledging a tenth of all he received (Genesis 28:20-22). Under the Law, Moses codified the tithe as holy unto the Lord (Leviticus 27:30).

And in the New Testament, Jesus affirmed the practice, urging the Pharisees to continue tithing but not neglect justice, mercy, and faith (Matthew 23:23).

What this means is that tithing is not a legalistic burden but a timeless covenant response. When you tithe, you say with your substance, "God, You are first. I trust You. I honor You." And in return, He opens heaven over your life, and causes your endeavors to flourish.

2. Offerings

Offerings are a powerful expression of worship that go beyond the tithe. While the tithe is a set portion that belongs to God, offerings are voluntary gifts that include anything given over and above the tithe. They are not mandated by a fixed percentage but are given freely, as acts of love, gratitude, reverence, and trust. They are a way of saying, "Lord, I love you so much that I don't just obey You, by returning what is Yours, I give from what is mine because I trust You completely."

The story of the widow in Mark 12:41–44 is a striking example. She could have given a tenth of her two small coins, but she gave everything and was recognized by Christ. Why? Because she gave, not as a matter of obligation but heartfelt devotion. This is why the Scripture exhorts, "*Remember this: Whoever sows sparingly will also reap sparingly, and whoever sows generously will also reap generously. Each of you should give what you have decided in your heart to give, not reluctantly or under compulsion, for God loves a cheerful giver. And God is able to bless you abundantly, so that in all things at all times, having all that you need, you will abound in every good work*" (2 Corinthians 9:6-8).

Offerings are meant to be joyful, intentional, and personal. They are not about pressure but passion. And when given cheerfully, they attract divine attention, as God responds with provision, protection, and peace.

Did you know that the Noahic covenant was provoked by Noah's gratitude offering? In Genesis 8:20–21, after the flood Noah built an altar and offered burnt sacrifices from every clean animal. The aroma pleased the Lord, and He responded by making a covenant never to curse the ground again. Noah's reverence moved God's heart for a transgenerational covenant. Your cheerful offerings to God can unlock blessings that will overflow to your future generations!

3. Firstfruits

Firstfruits giving is one of the most powerful expressions of honor and covenant in God's Kingdom. The practice appears throughout Scripture, beginning with the agricultural context of ancient Israel. Farmers were instructed to bring the first and best portion of their harvest to God - not after they had stored enough for themselves, but at the very beginning. This act demonstrated faith; they were giving before they knew how the rest of the harvest would turn out. It was a way of saying, "Lord, I trust You to bless what remains because I've honored You with what came first."

Proverbs 3:9–10 (KJV) captures this beautifully: "*Honour the LORD with thy substance, and with the firstfruits of all thine increase: so shall thy barns be filled with plenty, and thy presses shall burst out with new wine.*" This is a covenant promise. When you honor God with your firstfruits, He responds with abundance. Your barns (representing your storage, your provision, and your future) are filled. Your presses (symbolizing productivity and overflow) burst forth. The covenantal truth about firstfruits is, when you give the first, you secure the rest.

Firstfruits giving applies to any form of increase. It could be a new job, a salary raise, a business breakthrough, a new income stream, or even the beginning of a new year. It's simply about recognizing beginnings and dedicating them to God. In doing so, you invite Him into the journey, not just the destination.

In Exodus 23:19, God commands, "*Bring the best of the firstfruits of your soil to the house of the LORD your God…*" This shows that firstfruits are meant to be brought to God's house, not scattered or spent casually. They are sacred, set apart, and meant to be offered with intentionality.

Romans 11:16 (KJV) adds a spiritual layer to the principle: "*If the firstfruit be holy, the lump is also holy.*" In other words, what you do with the first affects the rest. When the beginning is consecrated, the remainder is blessed. This is why firstfruits giving is not just ceremonial but covenantal. It's a spiritual agreement that sets the tone for everything that follows.

Firstfruits also reflect gratitude. You're not waiting until you've "settled" before giving; you're giving immediately, joyfully, and reverently. It's a way of saying, "Lord, I recognize Your hand in this increase, and I return the best portion to You." It's not about legalism but love, honor, and trust. And when done in faith, it unlocks uncommon favor and breakthrough.

4. **Giving to the Needy**

Giving to the poor, the needy, and the vulnerable is also a powerful covenant investment because it reflects God's compassion, mercy and justice. Proverbs 19:17 (KJV) says, *"He that hath pity upon the poor lendeth unto the LORD; and that which he hath given will he pay him again."*

Isn't this amazing? God says when you give to the poor, He treats it as a loan to Himself. Wow! And unlike human borrowers, God always repays, with superabundant interest.

Christ also highlighted this truth in Matthew 6:3–4 (NLT), "*But when you give to someone in need, don't let your left hand know what your right hand is doing. Give your gifts in private, and your Father, who sees everything, will reward you.*"

One of the most striking demonstrations of this is the case of Cornelius, a Roman centurion described in Acts 10:1–4. Though a Gentile, Cornelius was devout and generous. The angel who appeared to him said, "*Your prayers and gifts to the poor have come up as a memorial offering before God.*" His almsgiving acts were recorded in heaven. And this opened the door for a divine visitation upon him and his household.

You may not be able to build a school or feed a thousand people today, but every time you respond to the needs around you, especially widows and orphans (James 1:27), you are sowing into divine recompense. Covenant givers do not ignore suffering. They make room for mercy in their budgets, and God makes room for abundance in their lives.

5. Giving to God's Ministers

Giving to God's ministers is a deeply spiritual but often overlooked form of covenant giving. It is not about paying for services rendered but honoring the vessels through whom God pours out His word, wisdom, and grace. When you sow into the life of a minister or anointed servant of God, you are not just giving to a person but also connecting to the spiritual authority and grace that rests upon their life and ministry.

The story of the Shunammite woman in 2 Kings 4:8–17 is a powerful example. She noticed that Elisha, a prophet of God, frequently passed by her home. Instead of ignoring him, she chose to honor him by preparing meals and eventually building a furnished room for him to rest. She recognized Elisha as a holy man of God and responded with hospitality and honor. In return, Elisha released a prophetic word that reversed her barrenness and brought her a son. Her giving opened the door to a miracle that money alone could never buy.

Galatians 6:6 (NLT) reinforces this principle: "*Those who are taught the word of God should provide for their teachers, sharing all good things with them.*" Notice that this is not a suggestion but an instruction. When you receive spiritual nourishment, it is required that you respond with material support. It's a way of saying, "I value what you carry, and I honor the grace that flows through you."

The importance of this covenantal giving is further emphasized in 1 Corinthians 9:14: "*The Lord has commanded that those who preach the gospel should receive their living from the gospel.*" Ministers of the gospel often pour out their lives in service, prayer, teaching, and counsel.

Supporting them is a combination of kindness and Kingdom partnership. It allows them to focus on the work of ministry without distraction, while positioning you for long-term blessings through the spiritual harvest they are cultivating.

6. Building God's House

Building for the Lord is perhaps the greatest demonstration of covenant giving. While the world may celebrate investments in stocks, real estate, or business ventures, none of these can compare to the eternal value of building for the Lord. Whenever you build or contribute to building for God - whether it's a church, a house of prayer, a mission center, or any space dedicated to advancing His work - you are laying foundations that will reverberate into eternity. Banks may offer interest, but God offers lasting influence, favor, and legacy.

Scripture is filled with examples of individuals who built for God and received extraordinary blessings in return. One of the most remarkable is Solomon. He poured out his resources to build and dedicate a dwelling place for God in a demonstration of extravagant honor. And what happened next? God appeared to him, affirmed his throne, and made a covenant of His perpetual presence (2 Chronicles 7).

When you build or furnish God's house, you initiate blessings that not only distinguish you but also flow into your children and grandchildren. You attract supernatural encounters, because God honors those who honor Him.

Consider the Roman centurion in Luke 7. He wasn't even a Jew, yet he built a synagogue for the Jewish people. And when his servant was sick, even the religious leaders pleaded with Jesus on his behalf, saying, "*This man deserves to have you do this, because he loves our nation and has built our synagogue*" (Luke 7:4-5). His generosity had created spiritual capital, which yielded massive dividends for him, long after he had made the investment.

So, know this: by investing in God's house, you are investing in something eternal. And the return is both exponential and generational.

7. Giving to Your Parents

Giving to your parents may seem like just a cultural or moral gesture but it is far more than that. It is a divine command with a covenant promise attached. Ephesians 6:2–3 reminds us, *"Honor your father and mother"—which is the first commandment with a promise— "so that it may go well with you and that you may enjoy long life on the earth."*

This is a spiritual law. When you honor your parents, especially through material support, you activate all-round prosperity and longevity.

Many people struggle silently in life, not because they lack talent or opportunity, but because they have dishonored the wombs and voices that birthed and nurtured them. Honor is not just about words but about action. And one of the most tangible ways to act out honor is through giving. When you make room for your parents in your budget, God makes room for abundance in your life. When you care for those who once cared for you, heaven responds with favor and protection over you.

Joseph is a powerful example here. In Genesis 45:21–27, after revealing his identity to his brothers, Joseph sent wagons, provisions, and gifts to bring his father Jacob to Egypt. And when Jacob arrived, Joseph cared for him with dignity and love until his final breath. And what did Jacob do in return? He spent his dying moments blessing Joseph's sons, Ephraim and Manasseh, securing their place in Israel's future. Joseph's honor unlocked generational blessing.

Jesus Himself affirmed the importance of caring for parents. In Mark 7:9–13, He rebuked the Pharisees for using religious excuses to avoid supporting their parents financially. He made it clear that true devotion to God includes honoring one's father and mother, not just in speech, but in substance.

Therefore, stop seeing giving to your parents as a mere obligation and start seeing it as an opportunity for covenantal blessings. Whether it's monthly support, medical care, housing, or simply consistent attention, your giving is a covenant seed that God continually remembers and rewards!

LET THE GENERATIONAL INVESTMENT BEGIN

The revelations we have received so far from this chapter point to one truth: what you cheerfully give to God in obedience faith never leaves your life; it enters your future and multiplies. It becomes a divine currency that speaks for you in difficult seasons, attracts favor, and shields you in adversity. The covenant speaks even when your strength fails.

Psalm 112:9–10 (KJV) captures this well: *"He hath dispersed, he hath given to the poor; his righteousness endureth for ever; his horn shall be exalted with honor…"* Covenant givers don't fade; they flourish. So, begin right away. Engage in covenant giving, not as a duty but as a lifestyle. Give with faith and joy. And watch as God responds with His power, favor, and abundance for you and the generations that follow.

7

EMBRACE YOUR COVENANT RIGHT AND RESPONSIBILITY TO STAY DEBT-FREE

"I believe that through knowledge and discipline, financial peace is possible for all of us."

— Dave Ramsey

Debt is one of the most common causes of financial bondage, and sadly, believers sometimes find themselves trapped in its chains like the rest of humanity. The Bible minces no words in saying that *"the rich ruleth over the poor, and the borrower is servant to the lender"* (Proverbs 22:7). This means that debt is not just a financial matter but a form of servitude. It compels you to structure your life around repayment schedules, interest rates, and obligations to creditors rather than the freedom to serve God "*without fear, in holiness and righteousness*" all the days of your life (Luke 1:74-75).

Yet the Word of God makes it abundantly clear that freedom from debt is part of the covenant blessing available to His children. As we have established so far, from Genesis to Revelation, God's desire is to see His people prosper in such a way that we are not enslaved by financial obligations but equipped to fund Kingdom purposes, influence our communities and nations, as well as leave lasting legacies.

This is a belief and principle you must embrace in totality to flourish in Kingdom prosperity.

DEBT IS NOT A FLEX

Ironically, we live in a society that normalizes and even glamorizes borrowing. Loans, credit cards, and buy-now-pay-later schemes are packaged as incredible and indispensable offers. But the Kingdom culture is different. God specifically promises us in Deuteronomy 28:12: *"The LORD shall open unto thee his good treasure, the heaven to give the rain unto thy land in his season, and to bless all the work of thine hand: and thou shalt lend unto many nations, and thou shalt not borrow."* The message is clear: borrowing is not the identity of God's children; lending is.

However, rejecting borrowing does not mean refusing all financial instruments. For example, leveraging credit to expand a well-structured business can sometimes be wise. But the danger lies in adopting borrowing as a lifestyle or shortcut to prosperity. Living perpetually in debt is living beneath your covenant heritage. Paul's admonition in 1 Corinthians 7:23 (NIV) is striking here: *"...Do not become slaves of human beings."* Every time you become enslaved to debt, you voluntarily step back under servitude. God's will is that you live free, not bound.

THE WIDOW'S EMANCIPATION

Look again at the case of the widow whose prophet-husband died in debt. It shows how devastating the weight of debt can be: "*A certain woman of the wives of the sons of the prophets cried out to Elisha, saying, "Your servant my husband is dead, and you know that your servant feared the LORD. And the creditor is coming to take my two sons to be his slaves." So Elisha said to her, "What shall I do for you? Tell me, what do you have in the house?" And she said, "Your maidservant has nothing in the house but a jar of oil." Then he said, "Go, borrow vessels from everywhere, from all your neighbors—empty vessels; do not gather just a few. And when you have come in, you shall shut the door behind you and your sons; then pour it into all those vessels, and set aside the full ones." So she went from him and shut the door behind her and her sons, who brought the vessels to her; and she poured it out. Now it came to pass, when the vessels were full, that she said to her son, "Bring me another vessel." And he said to her, "There is not another vessel." So the oil ceased. Then she came and told the man of God. And he said, "Go, sell the oil and pay your debt; and you and your sons live on the rest*" (2 Kings 4:1-7).

This passage contains so much revelation about debt-free Kingdom living. First, it shows that debt does not die with the debtor; it can enslave generations after that. It does not just drain your wallet; it enslaves your future. It ties down your dreams, dictates your decisions, and often leaves you anxious rather than free.

The narrative also shows that while the late prophet feared God, he lacked understanding of how to operate in covenant provision. Fear of God without knowledge of covenant rights and responsibilities can still result in avoidable bondage. His widow, however, demonstrated covenant knowledge and wisdom. She cried out to Prophet Elisha, who opened her eyes to a covenant solution: the little jar of oil in her house. Through obedience, diligence, and faith, her oil multiplied until she had enough to pay the debt and live in abundance: *"Go, sell the oil, and pay thy debt, and live thou and thy children of the rest"* (2 Kings 4:7).

FREEDOM FROM DEBT

The happy ending of the widow's story further reminds us that debt is not God's plan for His people. We are destined to walk in freedom, abundance, and responsibility. This is why God provides creative strategies and supernatural supply to bring us out of financial bondage.

Bear in mind that your freedom from debt is not merely a financial principle but a covenant right sealed in Christ. Paul declared in 2 Corinthians 8:9: *"For ye know the grace of our Lord Jesus Christ, that, though he was rich, yet for your sakes he became poor, that ye through his poverty might be rich."* The atoning work of Christ not only redeemed us from sin and sickness but also from the curse of lack and insufficiency. To live under constant debt is to live below the abundance secured in the covenant.

Romans 13:8 further highlights this calling: *"Owe no man any thing, but to love one another: for he that loveth another hath fulfilled the law."* Paul was not teaching legalism here but Kingdom culture. The believer's only debt should be the continual obligation of love, not the financial burdens that rob peace and weaken testimony. When you live free from debt, you testify to the sufficiency of God's provision and display a faith that the world cannot ignore.

Notice, however, that the miracle required the widow's participation; she had to gather vessels, pour the oil, and sell it. This reiterates the truth that prosperity does not fall out of the sky; it flows through obedience and wise stewardship.

YOU NEED KNOWLEDGE AND RESPONSIBILITY

Covenant rights are always matched with covenant responsibilities. Here is Hosea 4:6 again: *"My people are destroyed for lack of knowledge."* Debt often thrives where financial ignorance reigns.

This is where we must also take responsibility as believers. Many of us pray for prosperity but sign contracts we don't understand, spend beyond our means, or live without budgets. Knowledge of financial stewardship is as spiritual as prayer and fasting. Jesus Himself taught in Luke 16:11: *"If therefore ye have not been faithful in the unrighteous mammon, who will commit to your trust the true riches?"* True riches are spiritual, but God tests us with financial management first.

This is why believers must embrace practical wisdom. Understand compound interest. Learn the difference between liabilities (what drains resources) and assets (what creates value). Recognize that credit cards, payday loans, and unchecked borrowing are not tools of prosperity but traps of servitude. Dave Ramsey's reminder rings true: *"Debt is not a tool; it's a trap."*

Debt-free living demands responsible stewardship. The parable of the talents in Matthew 25 is not merely about spiritual gifts; it is about stewardship in all dimensions. The master rewarded the servants who multiplied what they were given, but condemned the one who buried his talent. Likewise, God expects us to multiply whatever resources He entrusts to us, whether time, money, or skills.

The widow in 2 Kings 4 discovered her "oil" was enough to liberate her. Many today also carry oil - gifts, ideas, and opportunities - that could wipe out their financial struggles if only they would steward them wisely. Consider Joseph: even as a slave in Potiphar's house and later as a prisoner in Egypt, he managed resources so faithfully that he was elevated to govern the wealth of a nation. He did not borrow his way into influence; he stewarded his way into greatness.

Budgeting, saving, avoiding waste, and planning ahead are all expressions of stewardship. Proverbs 21:20 highlights this: *"There is treasure to be desired and oil in the dwelling of the wise; but a foolish man spendeth it up."* Wise believers preserve resources; foolish ones squander them and sink into debt.

God's covenant promises are sure, but they demand our cooperation through practical obedience. Living debt-free requires prayerful dependence on God, yes, but also conscious discipline. The apostle Paul himself worked as a tentmaker so he would not be financially dependent on others (Acts 18:3). He modeled diligence, discipline, and balance.

Believers can follow this path today by creating budgets that reflect their priorities, practicing contentment (1 Timothy 6:6), and sowing faithfully into God's Kingdom. The principle of sowing and reaping assures us that generosity produces harvests (2 Corinthians 9:6–11). Debt keeps you from giving freely, but freedom from debt positions you to give joyfully and reap abundantly.

FROM BORROWERS TO LENDERS

The ultimate vision of Kingdom prosperity is not just escaping debt but rising as lenders and distributors of God's resources. Imagine the testimony of a believer who not only lives debt-free but also provides interest-free loans to struggling families, supports missionaries, and funds community projects. This is what Moses foresaw in Deuteronomy 15:6: *"For the LORD thy God blesseth thee, as he promised thee: and thou shalt lend unto many nations, but thou shalt not borrow."*

Nehemiah modeled this Kingdom posture when he personally loaned resources to his people without charging interest (Nehemiah 5:10–11). He lived above the culture of exploitation, choosing instead to reflect God's generosity. This is the picture of covenant prosperity; living so abundantly that you empower others rather than exploit them.

Psalm 112 paints this portrait clearly: *"A good man sheweth favour, and lendeth… He hath dispersed, he hath given to the poor; his righteousness endureth for ever; his horn shall be exalted with honour"* (vv. 5, 9). Kingdom wealth is not about hoarding; it is about lending, dispersing, and blessing.

Essentially, debt-free living is not just financial wisdom but Kingdom truth. It proves that God's covenant is real, that His promises are dependable, and that His children live by a higher economy. To live free of debt is to stand as a testimony that Christ's redemption is total, covering not only your soul but also your finances.

God wants us to be lenders, not borrowers; stewards, not squanderers; distributors, not dependents. As you embrace your covenant right and responsibilities to stay debt-free, you will rise into a new season of freedom, provision, and overflow in Jesus name.

8

P-U-S-H: PRAY UNTIL SOMETHING HAPPENS

"Prayer lays hold of God's plan and becomes the link between his will and its accomplishment on earth."

– Elisabeth Elliot

So far, we have explored the foundational truths and principles that drive Kingdom prosperity. Yet, there remains one indispensable key without which the journey to sustained prosperity becomes incomplete, even impossible. That key is prayer.

Truth is, no matter how faithfully you apply the other principles, there are realms you may never enter and forces you may never overcome without a consistent life of prayer, and sometimes, fasting. While the other principles may help to unlock heaven, it is prayer that clears the skies, pushes back resistance, and calls down the showers.

You can also consider prayer as the engine that drives covenant wealth into manifestation. It is the power line that connects your efforts to Heaven's energy grid. It is the force that activates the promises, dismantles resistance, protects the harvest, and preserves the soul of the prosperous.

Again, prayer can be seen as the watering of all the other seeds you are sowing. Remember what Apostle Paul told the Corinthians about how increase is activated? "*I have planted, Apollos watered; but God gave the increase*" (1 Corinthians 3:6). Yes, the sowing had been done but between the sowing and the increase or reaping, the watering is critical.

Consider also the example of Abraham in Genesis 15. God had made a covenant with Abraham, promising him descendants as numerous as the stars and land for his inheritance. To seal this covenant, Abraham was instructed to prepare a sacrificial offering: a heifer, a goat, a ram, a dove, and a pigeon. He obeyed, laid the pieces before the Lord, and waited. But then something strange happened. Verse 11 says, *"Then birds of prey came down on the carcasses, but Abram drove them away."*

This is very instructive. Abraham had made the offering, but before the covenant could be sealed and the promise fulfilled, "birds of prey", which some versions describe as "vultures" came to devour the sacrifice. Abraham had to actively guard his offering. He didn't just give; he fought to protect what he had given, so that the expected result could manifest.

This is a picture of spiritual reality. Many believers sow sincerely and sacrificially but they stop there. They assume that giving alone guarantees breakthrough. Yet, just like Abraham, after the offering is made, spiritual vultures sometimes appear. These are forces that seek to consume the seed before it produces a harvest.

If Abraham had not driven the vultures away, the offering would have been desecrated. The covenant would have been compromised. The promise would have been delayed. This is why prayer after giving is non-negotiable.

Let's go into the details.

WHY WE MUST PRAY

1. Prayer activates divine promises

God's promises are not always automatically activated. He declares His will, but He expects us to engage it. He reveals this in Ezekiel 36:37 after giving some promises to the Israelites: *"Thus saith the Lord GOD; I will yet for this be enquired of by the house of Israel, to do it for them."* In other words, *"I've promised, but you must still ask."* This is why James 4:2 says, *"You do not have because you do not ask God"*. And Matthew 7:7 says, *"Ask, and it will be given to you; seek, and you will find; knock, and the door will be opened to you."*

Consider the deliverance of the Israelites from the captivity of Egypt. Even though God had promised it several years earlier and the set time had arrived, God told Moses that the activation began because "*I have heard them crying out because of their slave drivers, and I am concerned about their suffering*" (Exodus 3:7). Sometimes, things may not change if we do not express the desire for them to change. If you feel comfortable with poverty, God may not impose prosperity on you.

In 1 Kings 18 also, we are told that after God had already declared that rain would return to Israel, Elijah didn't wait passively for the manifestation. He climbed Mount Carmel, bowed low, and prayed earnestly, not once but seven times. Only then did the cloud appear. The promise was real. But it was prayer that pulled it into the natural realm.

Throughout Scripture, we see other men and women of God contending for their prophetic destinies through prayer. Jacob had to prevail in prayer to step into his true destiny (Genesis 32:22-32); Hannah had to pray for Samuel to be born even though God had said none would be barren; and Jabez had to pray for his blessing to manifest (1 Chronicles 4:9-10).

Kingdom prosperity is no different. God may promise you abundance, but you need to pray, not only because it shows your desire but because it demonstrates your firm belief in God's faithfulness and His ability to do what He has said.

2. Prayer unlocks divine ideas and instructions

Kingdom prosperity is often hidden in divine revelations and instructions. Sometimes all you need is not more capital, but clearer vision. God can give you an idea that will lift you from poverty to influence.

It was through divine revelation that Jacob received the idea of using speckled rods to influence the breeding of cattle, and God increased him mightily (Genesis 30:37–43). Peter and the rest had toiled all night and caught nothing, until a divine instruction came: *"Cast the net on the right side of the ship."* The result was a net-breaking catch (John 21:6).

George Washington Carver is widely remembered today as a great American agricultural scientist, inventor and educator. He is best known for his groundbreaking work with peanuts, sweet potatoes, and other crops. He developed over 300 products from peanuts alone, including food items, cosmetics, paints, and industrial materials. Interestingly, the secret of these achievements which greatly transformed America's agricultural economy was not his scientific background but his prayer life.

He once famously revealed, "No books ever go into my laboratory. The thing I am to do and the way of doing it are revealed to me. I never have to grope for methods. The method is revealed to me the moment I am inspired to create something new."

These examples show that prosperity is more often a product of revelation than perspiration, and that revelation is unlocked mostly by prayer!

3. Prayer attracts destiny connections and favor

Sometimes, what unlocks Kingdom prosperity is not just your preparation but divine positioning. Prayer makes this happen. It is the invisible hand that guides you into rooms you didn't apply to enter, conversations you weren't scheduled to have, and relationships you couldn't have orchestrated.

When you pray, you're not just asking for provision; you're aligning yourself with God's network of influence. You may not know the right people, but when you know the right God, He moves the hearts of kings, gatekeepers, and helpers on your behalf. Proverbs 21:1

says, "*The king's heart is in the hand of the Lord; like the rivers of water, He turns it wherever He wishes.*" Prayer activates that turning.

4. Prayer breaks evil yokes and patterns

Some poverty problems are spiritual in origin. Generational curses, hidden covenants, or satanic embargoes can hinder even the most gifted and hardworking individuals. Jabez understood this. Though "more honourable than his brethren," he bore a name linked with sorrow, and it limited his destiny. But he didn't resign to fate. He prayed: *"Oh that thou wouldest bless me indeed, and enlarge my coast, and that thine hand might be with me…"* (1 Chronicles 4:10) And God answered him.

Prayer breaks what logic cannot explain. It uproots demonic patterns and dislodges ancestral barriers. And sometimes, prayer alone is not enough. Jesus told His disciples, *"This kind goeth not out but by prayer and fasting"* (Matthew 17:21). There are levels of bondage that demand a higher consecration to shatter. Fasting subdues the flesh and sharpens spiritual perception. When coupled with persistent prayer, it becomes a weapon of mass destruction against poverty and stagnation.

5. Prayer dislodges satanic manipulations

John 10:10 says, "*The thief comes only to steal and kill and destroy…*" Just as God wants His people prosperous, so also does Satan wants us shackled by lack. One way he tries to do this is to limit, hinder or sabotage our harvest.

I already showed you the example of Abraham and the "birds of prey" that wanted to frustrate his blessing. But there is an even more direct example to show that the enemy isn't interested in seeing you enjoy a good harvest for all your sowing. In Matthew 13:24-25, Jesus told a revealing parable: "*The kingdom of heaven is like a man who sowed good seed in his field; but while men slept, his enemy came and sowed tares among the wheat and went his way.*"

That's how the enemy operates. He may not be able to prevent you from sowing, but he will do all he can to sabotage your harvest. Tares can come in form of delays or devourers - health crises, betrayal, bad investments, legal issues etc. And while God has promised to rebuke them for us, He still commands us to "watch and pray".

Jacob shared his own testimony of victory over sabotage thus: "*You know that I've worked for your father with all my strength, yet your father has cheated me by changing my wages ten times. However, God has not allowed him to harm me.*" (Genesis 31:6-7). Paul also reminds us in Ephesians

6:12 (NKJV) that "*we do not wrestle against flesh and blood, but against principalities, against powers, against the rulers of the darkness of this age, against spiritual hosts of wickedness in the heavenly places.*" Prayer is how we wrestle. Without prayer, your prosperity can become vulnerable to visible and invisible sabotage. That promotion, that business growth, that idea that just began to flourish—none of it can be sustained without divine protection, and prayer is the shield.

6. Prayer prevents compromise and complacency

As we've already seen, one of the greatest spiritual risks of abundance is forgetting who brought you there, forgetting why you were blessed, and forgetting the posture that positioned you for increase in the first place. This is why you must keep the altar of prayer burning. Patriarchs like Abraham always built an altar of worship wherever they went. They knew that prosperity, when not constantly anchored in prayer, can quietly shift the heart from dependence to self-sufficiency.

Deuteronomy 8:17–18 (KJV) warns: "*And thou say in thine heart, My power and the might of mine hand hath gotten me this wealth. But thou shalt remember the Lord thy God: for it is he that giveth thee power to get wealth.*"

Prayer reminds you, day by day, that the true source of your wealth is not your hand but God's. Some people lose what they've gained because they stop praying once they prosper. They prayed fervently when they were in need, but once the breakthrough came, the altar grew cold. But prayer is not just what gets you there; it's what keeps you there. It's the spiritual maintenance that sustains the blessing and protects your heart from drifting.

PATTERN OF KINGDOM PROSPERITY PRAYER

The kind of prayer that activates and secures Kingdom prosperity has three key attributes.

1. It is Covenant-Aligned

Your prayer must be grounded in God's covenant promises. Don't beg as if you're approaching a reluctant God. Approach boldly, knowing you are in a covenant sealed by the blood of Jesus. Hebrews 4:16 urges us: "*Let us therefore come boldly unto the throne of grace.*"

Pray with Scripture. Declare what God has said. If you're a tither and giver, remind God (not arrogantly, but covenant-consciously) of His word in Malachi 3:10–12. You can say, "Lord, rebuke the devourer for my sake. Open the windows of Heaven." God is not insulted when you pray His promises back to Him. He is honored.

2. It is Purpose-Driven

We have established that Kingdom prosperity is not for personal gratification but Kingdom impact. When your motives align with God's agenda, your prayers gain weight. James 4:3 says, "*You ask and do not receive, because you ask amiss, that you may spend it on your pleasures.*"

So, don't just pray for money; pray for Kingdom impact. Pray for the ability to bless others, for wisdom to manage resources well, for doors that will position you as a light in the world of darkness and suffering. When you align your requests with God's purposes, Heaven listens.

3. It is Persistent

Jesus said in Luke 18:1, "*Men ought always to pray and not to faint.*" Some financial doors don't open with one knock. Some strongholds require prolonged wrestling. There are times when fasting must accompany your prayer to break the grip of spiritual resistance.

Isaiah 58:6 declares the kind of fast God honors: "*to loose the bands of wickedness, to undo the heavy burdens, and to let the oppressed go free.*" If you are facing delay, stagnation, or unexplained hardship, consider fasting alongside your prayers.

With faith, faithfulness and persistence, your breakthrough into Kingdom prosperity will come.

FINAL WORDS: FROM REVELATION TO MANIFESTATION

I believe you have been richly blessed by the revelations in this book. Together, we have explored both the spiritual and practical foundations of Kingdom prosperity. We have learned that God delights in prospering His children; but He does not do so haphazardly. His blessings follow covenant, purpose, obedience, and faith. To prosper in God's Kingdom is to submit to His authority in all things; it is to believe the truth of His Word, to sow diligently, give faithfully, and pray fervently.

We have also seen that prosperity is not an indulgence but a stewardship. What God places in our hands is never for us alone. Abraham was blessed to be a blessing. Joseph was elevated to preserve a nation. Esther's royal position became a platform for divine intervention. So it must be with us. Kingdom prosperity flows through vessels who are willing to serve, sacrifice, and remain surrendered.

Now, the responsibility shifts to you. It is not enough to know the truth; you must act on it. As James reminds us, we are called to be doers of the Word, not hearers only, deceiving ourselves (James 1:22). The truths shared in this book will remain dormant unless they are activated by faith, practiced through obedience, and sustained by commitment.

Let the Word of God break every limiting belief and renew your mind. Let prayer stir your spirit until God's desire and purpose for your prosperity become reality. Let the altar of your heart remain burning as you engage God for deeper understanding and greater elevation.

Above all, remember that the most dangerous kind of success is the kind that leads a person away from God. True Kingdom prosperity will always draw you closer to Him. It will make you love more deeply, give more sacrificially, and serve more faithfully. It humbles, even as it honors. It multiplies resources, but also multiplies responsibility.

As you close this book, may you open a new chapter in your life. May you rise with fresh conviction and renewed vision, not just for financial increase, but for spiritual maturity, impactful living, and generational legacy. May you reject every limiting lie and embrace the truth of abundance. May you prosper, even as your soul prospers. And may your prosperity produce a massive trail of Kingdom impact.

www.ingramcontent.com/pod-product-compliance
Lightning Source LLC
LaVergne TN
LVHW010930110826
845149LV00013B/2536

* 9 7 8 1 9 6 5 5 9 3 8 2 0 *